Leadership

Dynamics

Building Effective Teams

How to build groups with vision and influence for a preferable future!

By Bob Perry

Table of Contents

Table of Illustrations

Introduction

"Where there is no guidance, a people fall;
but in an abundance of counselors there is safety."
SOLOMON

Solomon's proverb speaks about the enduring role of leadership. A void of leadership and guidance results in aimlessness, failure, and sometimes disaster for a group. Organizational leadership is a shared activity. It depends on many people throughout an organization to provide direction, purpose, influence, vision, and security for a group.

This book focuses on developing "leaders" rather than "the leader." Organizations depend on good leadership throughout their structure. The ability to understand people and groups is essential to achieving success.

The word dynamic is defined as a branch of mechanics concerned with the effects of force on the motion of a body, object, or system. Thinking dynamically means analyzing the driving forces and controlling forces to influence them in a predictable way. A dynamic is how something works. This book explains complex interpersonal and organizational situations by defining them in mechanical or systematic terms.

Leadership Dynamics is organized into four sections:
- Creating Vision and Influence
- Transforming Ideas Into Results
- Solving Problems While Managing Change
- Dealing with Difficult People

Chapters, although interrelated around the theme of leadership dynamics, can be used independently. Pick and choose the areas that interest you the most. Readers will enjoy, comprehend, and learn better if they are involved and interested in the material. I hope the ideas presented in this book develop your thoughts about leadership and help you become more effective in working with groups of people and building effective teams.

This book uses the models, or dynamics, to help build your ability to see the present more clearly and influence a preferable future for yourself and your organization. The purpose of *Leadership Dynamics: Building Effective Teams* is to help you develop your leadership capabilities to effectively deal with other people.

Organizations are usually composed of many smaller groups of varying size and complexity. Untangling these complex interactions to determine what is happening and what might happen next is the challenge in leadership. *Leadership Dynamics: Building Effective Teams* uses a simple method of systematically looking at driving forces and controlling forces to understand and influence the behavior of groups.

The challenges of leadership and the dynamics at work in groups are the same for a business organization, a volunteer group, a work team, a school, an agency, or even a church group. Although all of these groups have different goals, objectives, and missions, they all have a need for different personalities with differing ideas to work effectively together. All groups need leaders with vision and influence to move them toward success. *Leadership Dynamics: Building Effective Teams* is a tool to help individuals develop leadership capability and to help groups succeed.

PART I

Creating Vision and Influence

The essential ingredients of leadership include vision and influence. Creating vision begins with a clear perspective of the present reality. Creating a vision of the current reality takes courage since we often have to deal with brutal facts instead of our comfortable illusions. Having a clear vision of the current reality facing a group is like having a compass and a map in the forest. It provides direction and control to leadership even though the final destination may be out of view.

Influence is the force behind leadership. The ability to influence other people and get them moving is a primary responsibility of leadership. Whether you are leading a small group or an entire organization, improving your leadership skills will make you more valuable and help your group achieve more.

Chapter 1
Dynamic of Leadership:
Driving Force versus Controlling Force

"Objects in motion stay in motion and objects at rest stay at rest."

Sir Isaac Newton

What would it be like to see the future…to predict outcomes of events before they occur? Imagine the power of knowing what is likely to happen five years or even five hours into the future! Learning to examine yesterday's events and today's reality to predict probable outcomes for tomorrow is a powerful tool in leadership and in life. Creating this type of predictive vision requires two things: a clear perspective of the present reality and the ability to influence future actions.

In physics, the center of gravity is an infinitely small point upon which an object can be balanced. Almost anything can be balanced regardless of size or shape, if the center of gravity can be identified. Since the center of gravity can be quite small, balancing an object requires constant adjustment to achieve equilibrium.

Balance is essential in natural science. The universe is a balance between mass and motion. Our earth is balanced between the velocity of movement and gravity to keep an orbit around the sun to sustain life. There is a balance in nature keeping ecological systems thriving. When imbalance occurs, species suffer and nature goes into chaos until it is able to rebalance itself.

Many aspects of human experience require balance.

Many aspects of human experience require balance. Nutritionally we need a balanced diet. Financially we need a balanced checkbook. Socially we must balance priorities, time, and personalities to achieve a level of fulfillment in life.

We continually make adjustments in behavior trying to achieve balance. A variety of interpersonal factors must balance to achieve success.

For instance, a person must balance:

- **passion with pragmatism**
- **assertiveness with tactfulness**
- **risk with safety**
- **authority with responsibility**
- **opportunities with available resources**
- **contentment with creativity.**

The great physicist Sir Isaac Newton observed phenomena in nature and realized invisible forces were at work affecting physical objects in the universe. As a mathematician, he devised theories and formulas to help explain and predict the motion of objects. Newton's contributions to science described the working of a large part of inanimate nature in mathematical terms and suggested the remainder could be understood in a similar manner. These principles of motion and the effects of force are fundamental in understanding how things work in the physical world.

Dynamics is a branch of mechanics focused on the effect of force on objects. The internal combustion engine, for example, harnesses the force of an explosion to control the cause and effect making engine parts move in a predictable way. Simply put, **a dynamic is how things work.**

Thinking dynamically analyzes driving forces and controlling forces to influence them in a predictable way.

Dynamics, however, are at work in much more than just mechanics. Dynamics occur in interpersonal relationships and in intra-personal reasoning.

Leadership dynamics affect the social, intellectual, and moral forces producing activity and change. Many forces affect events in the psychology of individuals and the sociology of groups. Effectively working through interpersonal situations requires analyzing these forces and their effect. Thinking dynamically involves analyzing driving forces and controlling forces to influence them in a predictable way.

Driving Force and Controlling Force

Force is the invisible entity affecting the motion of objects. The two basic dynamics are at work in most situations: *driving force* and *controlling force*. Driving force produces intensity of motion while controlling force determines direction.

The dynamic of driving and controlling forces can be easily identified and analyzed in physical objects. For example, a freight train has the driving force of the locomotive, which moves the train forward with intensity of motion. Steel tracks provide controlling force dictating the direction of the forward momentum. The route of the train can be determined by simply looking at the controlling force or the direction of the track. If the tracks are worn, weak, or have sharp turns, the locomotive will have to travel more slowly and cautiously by decreasing the driving force. If the controlling force of the tracks is overpowered by the driving force, chaos, destruction, and possibly tragedy results. On the other hand, if the driving force is too weak to overcome the friction between the wheels and the tracks the train will stagnate and stop. Driving force and controlling force must be in balance for normal operations. The two forces are being continuously adjusted to achieve the desired balance.

Balancing driving force and controlling force is the essence of auto racing. The noise and speed of the cars in this sport is amazing as they travel at unbelievable speeds while maneuvering all over the track. Tires on a family car may go 50,000 miles or more, but a race team changes tires several times during a 500-mile race. It takes valuable time to switch tires and time is everything in racing. Racecar tires, however, are wide and soft. Tires are designed to stick to the track; not last a long-time. The powerful engine provides the driving force on these machines, but the tires become the all-important controlling force.

Drivers balance these two forces constantly to have success in a race. Their goal is to maximize the speed of the car and judge its momentum before going into the turns of the racetrack. The driver must know his driving force (speed) as compared to the controlling force (traction) to guide the car to the finish line in the fastest time possible. If the driver has too much speed, he will lose control, spin out, or crash into the wall. The race team is continuously determining the cost verses the benefit of balancing the two forces. Taking the time to put on fresh tires costs time, but racing with a slower driving force when the slick tires are not providing enough controlling force may lose more time.

Leaders of organizations do much the same thing to help groups reach desired objectives. The strength of the driving force must be in balance with the controlling forces. When controlling forces are not strong enough to contain the driving force of the new initiatives, their capacity needs to be increased or the driving force of the group must be decreased to avoid putting the organization into chaos. Leaders of groups are always balancing the driving forces with the controlling forces for maximum efficiency.

Driving forces and controlling forces are also at work in the interpersonal interaction of people. Organizational planning illustrates these two forces working together to affect the activities of a group. Planning begins with the driving forces of desires, ideals, values, and a vision of the preferred future. These forces can be strong motivators, particularly in entrepreneurial organizations. These strong driving forces, however, are tempered with the controlling forces of available resources and the reality of the current situation.

A leader of a business organization might aspire to develop new products, expand market share, or open new markets. The driving force of these desires will be controlled or constrained by the realities of the organization's capacities, resources, and abilities. If the driving force is greater than the controlling force, the group will be pushed into a chaotic situation. If the driving force is much less than the capacity of the controlling force however, the organization stagnates and fails to reach its full potential.

Leadership is part science and part art. Proven theories and practices achieve results, but sometimes a leader relies on instincts to determine the magnitude of the driving force and strength of controlling forces.

Driving force and controlling force are perhaps the two most powerful tools available to influence future events.

Understanding the dynamics of force on a group and learning how to work with and control that force is part of the art of leadership. Some leaders learn to be more observant and understanding while others have a natural aptitude for seeing and using these forces to reach their objectives.

Driving force and controlling force are perhaps the two most powerful tools available to influence future events. By increasing or decreasing the magnitude of these two forces, a leader can successfully impact performance and outcomes. A stagnate group may need more driving force in the form of motivation, encouragement, or enticement. A stagnate group may also need the bureaucratic controlling forces reduced to encourage movement. In contrast, a group making too many mistakes and embroiled in conflict may need more controlling force in the form of rules, policy, and more careful monitoring.

Most effective leaders have a talent for understanding the personalities and characteristics of people. They realize the power of diversity. They understand how to utilize individual strengths and weaknesses. These leaders believe no individual is perfect, but a team can have a more complete vision of reality. They have the ability to position people as "role-players" to allow them to succeed individually and organizationally based on their strengths. Groups or individuals have differing personalities, some of which are driving forces while others are controlling forces.

For example, the attributes of an optimistic person and a pragmatic person can combine to provide a positive balance of driving force and controlling force. Passionate, optimistic people can provide a strong driving force in a group. As Ralph Waldo Emerson once said, "Passion, though a bad regulator, is a powerful spring." Passionate and optimistic people are generally productive and driven, but they often overlook obvious obstacles and barriers. A more pragmatic person added to the team, however, might provide important controlling force.

A group comprised totally of overly passionate people may be too aggressive and outstrip the needed controlling force. Adding some pragmatic people to the group may balance the effort. The practicality of these people may be able to point out pitfalls in a project. A group of pragmatic people on the other hand, may not accomplish as much when they lack the "can do" attitude of optimism. The optimistic person will be a useful driving force but the pragmatic person may be an equally valuable controlling force. Good team builders find an optimum balance.

The motion picture "Patton," chronicling the World War II career of General George Patton, is a good example of the dynamic of force working in personalities. The supreme commander, General Eisenhower, is not seen in the movie although he is one of the key characters. Eisenhower uses Patton as the driving force many times in the story. Patton was a hard-charging fighter causing motion and commotion wherever he went. His driven personality is tempered and balanced by another character and contrasting personality, General Omar Bradley. Although the politics, intrigue, and personal dynamics of World War II generals are infinitely complex, in this instance Patton is portrayed as the driving force while Bradley provides the all-important controlling force.

In organizations, the controlling force can be established in a number of ways. In very small groups, a leader can sometimes "take the pulse" of the group and provide the controlling force. As groups get bigger however, this becomes more difficult. Many successful small businesses struggle to grow to their full potential because they outstrip the leader's ability to provide adequate controlling force.

As organizations grow, they need more stable controlling forces. Organizational policies, procedures, and established processes are how larger organizations provide controlling force for the many members. As these controlling forces are adopted and accepted by the group, they become part of the culture of the organization. Typically the larger the group, the more formal and detailed the controlling force becomes.

For larger organizations, this systemized controlling force can overwhelm the driving forces. Bureaucracy, a system of administration marked by rigid procedures, red tape, proliferation of paperwork, and deferred decision-making, is a term often associated with organizations having too much controlling force. Sometimes organizations attempt to overcome this strong controlling force by offering pay incentives, bonuses, or stronger directives from managers. The inability of large companies to balance the driving force of changing markets with the controlling force of bureaucracy is one reason small businesses periodically emerge to meet these rapidly changing markets. Numerous examples appear every year of once powerful companies in decline because of their own overwhelming controlling forces. By contrast, many more start-up organizations fail because they have too little controlling force. Learning to balance driving forces and controlling forces can be one of the best skills a leader can develop.

The momentum of the driving force is constantly changing, either accelerating or decelerating. The magnitude of the force must be judged and balanced with appropriate constraints and controlling force to affect positive outcomes for a group. Thinking dynamically requires observing, identifying, and analyzing the driving force and controlling force involved in situations. By learning to adjust these forces, a leader can dramatically influence the direction and vitality of a group of people.

Key Points

- As with physical objects, invisible forces are at work in the psychology of individuals and the sociology of groups.
- Driving force and controlling force work together in determining the outcome of events.
- Driving force and controlling force need to be in balance. Too much driving force creates chaos and confusion while too much controlling force results in stagnation and obsolescence.
- Leaders can affect the performance of groups by adjusting the driving forces and controlling forces involved in group interaction.

Chapter 2
Dynamic of Vision:
Seeing the Current Reality

"Having a vision of tomorrow requires a clear vision of today."

Having a vision for the future requires a clear vision of the present. Thinking dynamically (analyzing situations in terms of driving force and controlling force) leads to a better understanding of what is happening, why it is happening, and what might happen next. To forecast probable outcomes in the future, **it is absolutely necessary to see the realities of the current environment.**

Thinking dynamically is a methodology employed in many disciplines. A mathematician finds the unknown quantity of an equation by determining and understanding the known quantities. A meteorologist predicts weather by determining the current conditions and analyzing the known data to predict weather. An engineer analyzes information about mechanical and structural systems to determine how forces will likely react. A medical doctor observes the condition of the patient, combined with experience and knowledge to determine the health of the patient.

> Thinking dynamically is a methodology employed in many disciplines.

All of these professions depend on making calculations about unknown quantities by accurately seeing the current reality, collecting data, and combining that information with past experiences to understand the dynamics of driving force and controlling force. The ability to think dynamically begins by developing a vision of the current reality. It continues by understanding the dynamics in the situation to forecast future events.

Cause and effect is a fundamental phenomenon occurring in most aspects of human existence and all elements found in nature. Planet earth holds its critical orbit around the sun by the dynamic force of gravity. The tides of the ocean occur due to the dynamic force of the moon's orbit of the earth. The seasons change because there is a dynamic force at work related to the tilt of the earth. All of these natural phenomena happen because of cause and effect relationships.

In interpersonal interactions, the dynamic of a temperamental personality interacting with an emotional personality is obvious. There is no surprise when someone gets angry and someone ends up crying. Not all dynamics are so obvious.

Tornados are the most violent and destructive weather on the planet. The conditions producing a tornado exist when moist, warm air is trapped beneath a stable layer of cold, dry air. The warm, humid air moving up through the more stable cold air starts to spiral upward. Heat is released as the moisture it holds condenses. Winds at various levels of the atmosphere then rotate the updraft as it gains velocity. All of these meteorological factors working together can be the origin of a tornado.

These fierce storms are now more predictable because meteorologists have developed tools to measure the many factors, which may cause a tornado. They have learned to interpret these observations to predict likely storms. Meteorologists are able to issue watches and warnings letting people prepare for the damaging storms, which can avoid injury, and sometimes death.

Fortunately, a tornado does not develop every time the conditions say it might. Predicting the weather is a tricky business. It is a science considering many factors interacting rapidly with one another. The dynamics of any situation can be simple or complex depending on the number of variables interacting with each other. Most things, both physical and psychological, are affected by a variety of forces. An understanding of these invisible forces can help predict interpersonal dynamics influencing events.

As invisible physical forces affect physical objects, other invisible forces are also influencing the psychology of individuals and the sociology of groups. People are influenced by a wide variety of forces both internal and external. To think dynamically involves observation and analysis to determine what is happening and what might happen next. Thinking dynamically begins by developing a true and clear vision of the present reality.

CREATING VISION

Creating vision is fundamental to effectively influencing groups. People with vision are often thought to have special powers or abilities…a gift or extraordinary creativity to see the future. Creating vision, however, is a skill that can be learned, improved, and applied by using a structured approach.

Understanding the dynamic of a situation is simply an attempt to determine what is happening, why it is happening, and what might happen next. Having vision means thinking in terms of what is, what has been, and what might be. Knowing as much as possible about the current situation—developing the ability to see things the way they really are—is necessary in determining how things are likely to be. As the British historian Thomas Carlyle once wrote, "Our main business is not to see what lies dimly at a distance, but to do what lies clearly at hand." Having a vision of the future is predicated on having a clear understanding of the current reality.

People with a natural aptitude and insight for this type of inductive reasoning often seem like natural leaders since they have the ability to recognize what is really happening and make appropriate responses to positively influence current and future circumstances. Recognizing the dynamics at work in situations by learning to use a structured approach to analyze events can help increase

Objectively analyzing yesterday's events and today's trends can help influence tomorrow's

vision of the current reality. It leads to a better understanding of what is happening, why it is happening, and what might happen next. Objectively analyzing yesterday's events and today's trends can help influence tomorrow's outcomes.

The purpose of studying history is to help develop a better perspective of today's reality to help predict a likely future. As Winston Churchill explained, "The further backward you can look, the further forward you are likely to see." Tomorrow is inherent in today. Understanding the dynamics in situations today can help shed light on probable activities in the future. Thinking dynamically requires vision to observe reality and the ability to make predictions or calculated guesses about future events based on these observations.

JFK JR. AND THE TRAGEDY OF SPATIAL DISORIENTATION

Failure to see the current reality leads to errant decision-making and sometimes disastrous consequences. On July 16, 1999, 38 year old John F. Kennedy Jr. piloted a small plane from New York City toward Martha's Vineyard, Massachusetts that crashed into the Atlantic Ocean. Kennedy was a "visual flight rules" pilot without an instrument rating. The night of the flight, he was delayed, meaning he had to fly over the open ocean at night with hazy conditions.

A number of factors possibly led to this tragedy: the weather, the equipment, and even the pilot's inexperience. After an exhaustive investigation, the National Transportation Safety Board concluded that the biggest factor was a phenomenon known as **spatial disorientation**. Spatial disorientation is a strange and deadly phenomenon that can make a pilot believe up is down and down is up. It can make them think left is right and right is left. Your body tells you one thing while the instruments show something else is happening. The plane was descending at more than 4,700 feet per minute and most experts believed several critical moments passed before Kennedy realized he was in trouble.

Doctor Peter Salgo, an Aviation Medical Examiner said, "Pilots over a dark piece of water, at night, with haze, without visual references, are prone to illusions which can lead them to a graveyard spiral. These graveyard spirals can happen quickly. The rate of decent becomes astronomical, and recovering from one, once it's really established, especially if you are an inexperienced pilot, is very difficult if not impossible."[1]

Had Kennedy been instrument rated, had he been able to establish a vision of the current reality using those instruments, the tragedy might possibly have been avoided. Failing to see the current reality and developing the skill to find measures to help determine that reality can have disastrous effects. Effective leadership demands seeing the current reality in situations. Leaders must develop the tools and methodology to get past the clutter and confusion that becomes a barrier to vision.

---

[1] Discovery Channel, "Crashes", 2002

BARRIERS TO SEEING THE CURRENT REALITY

There are several challenges to seeing reality. Truth is often camouflaged among personal opinions, incomplete knowledge, and restricted understanding. Time, perspective, objectivity, and prejudice are some of the most common challenges in developing a clear vision of the present.

Time

In the summer of 2001, the 101st United States Open golf championship came to Southern Hills country club in Tulsa, Oklahoma. I had seen the U. S. Open when it was played at Tulsa in 1977 and was anxious for my two children to see the best players in the world play. We had tickets for Friday's second round. By midafternoon the walking, the heat, and the hills had taken their toll and we were looking for a place to sit in the shade.

We picked the bleachers behind the 5th green. These seats not only had a good view of the 5th hole but also had a great view of the par three 6th hole looking directly behind the tee box and toward its green. While watching groups come through, we heard cheers and groans from other parts of the course we could not see. Occasionally information was posted on the leaderboard and we would guess at what happened out of view.

Later in the afternoon, we saw Phil Mickleson make a hole-in-one on the par three 6th hole. We were sitting high enough in the bleachers to not only see the shot, but to see the hole. In fact, our view of the hole was probably better than his. The crowd roared and out of 40,000 spectators at the event, we had been part of the few hundred who actually saw the shot.

That night we drove home and immediately turned on the replay show to see the day's events. Sure enough, they showed Mickleson's shot. The program, a tape delay of the action as it was happening, demonstrated how little of the golf tournament we had actually seen! While we were watching the action on holes 5 and 6, play was occurring on 16 other holes. Seeing the action on television helped explain some of the groans and cheers we had heard through the afternoon.

While we could clearly see the play right in front of us, the noise and information from around the course was less clear. Sometimes we were reasonably accurate at determining what had happened, but often we did not know or made false assumptions.

In keeping up with the action in the golf tournament and trying to determine what was really happening, we relied on other information beyond what we could physically see. The cheers and groans of the gallery on other parts of the course was one tool we used in keeping up with the action. By taking a map of the golf course and the time sheet listing the player's schedule on course, we could determine what players were at which hole. A groan from the 12th hole, out of our view, meant someone had missed a shot. The intensity of the reaction indicated the importance of the shot and possibly the player making it.

The scoreboard or leaderboard was another tool in creating a vision of what was happening at the golf tournament. The leaderboard represented information about the score and play of the players. Leaderboard information, though factual, is still incomplete. It tells what has happened but not how it happened.

In determining how players were doing, we relied on yet another method of determining the truth by talking and listening to other members of the gallery. Other people had been on different parts of the course and had a different view of the action than we had. Getting the perspective from as many people as possible is a good way to determine the truth and reality in situations that are not directly observable. It is also a challenging method and requires skill and the ability extrapolate information.

Sometimes people we talked to were not eyewitnesses to the events. Many times, they were relaying information they had heard second and third hand. Some gallery members were not accurate in passing on information. They would get too excited about the action and subconsciously exaggerate the facts. A putt of 30 feet, which was made by a player, may become a putt of 60 feet when retold a few times.

Bias and preconceived opinions about players also affect the information people perceive. Getting the view from someone else and creating vision based on other people's perspective requires gathering a lot of information, then synthesizing that information based on experience, congruency, and consistency. The truth is usually there, but its exact location can be cloudy based on the opinions and ability of others to communicate. Time is always a barrier in creating vision. No human being is omnipotent or omnipresent. We must develop the ability to take partial information to find truth and reality.

Even with seats high above the action, and with an excellent view of two holes, the perspective was limited. I personally did not see Mickleson's ball go in the hole. I was watching the players putt on the fifth hole. What I actually saw was Phil Mickleson pumping his fist in the air after hearing the roar of the crowd. I was in position to see it, but the restriction of time (trying to watch two holes at once) became a barrier to clear vision of the present.

Many of the barriers we faced in seeing the golf tournament are similar to the vision barriers we face in real life. We were not seeing the whole golf tournament, only pieces of it restricted by perspective and time. In life, people constantly have to create vision and truth based on partial information. The time we spent at our location limited our ability to see other events happening at the same time. Watching the replay on television was like seeing things in hindsight. The replay showed the big picture of the golf tournament unrestricted by time or perspective. Of course, much more was happening than what was shown on television. The television people simply attempted to show the most important, most interesting, and most pertinent events on their broadcast.

Today is Yesterday's Tomorrow...
Yesterday's Tomorrow is Today...
Tomorrow's Yesterday is Today.

Time is a dimension constantly moving forward and continually restricting our ability to see everything happening. In creating a vision of the present, it is necessary to understand the challenges of time in determining reality. Time is a snapshot of the moment, which is a result of a series of past events and influences comprising that moment.

The inertia and momentum up to a specific point in time will continue. Nothing stays the same because time is constantly moving forward. Thinking dynamically will expand the awareness of the current reality to give insight in determining the momentum of the future.

Perspective

Perspective presents another challenge in seeing reality. Often people are too close to a situation to objectively analyze the reality. Take a coin and hold it about two inches from one eye while closing the other eye. If you have normal vision, you may be able to see the coin and possibly determine its value. Most people though, will not be able to see the date on the coin. The coin can be seen, but by being so close, it is impossible to see the details and all the information on the coin.

Being too close to events becomes a barrier to clearly seeing the details and the truth about what is actually happening. Taking the same coin and holding it further away makes it possible to see much better and to glean more information from it. The date can be clearly read and the denomination accurately determined. The coin can even be turned around to get even more information and perspective. To get a clearer view of a situation, it is often necessary to get further away from the action to gain the proper perspective.

My son played center on his freshman football team. I watched every game paying special attention to the middle of the offensive line. Most people watched the ball, but a parent focuses on their child. After games, when I would asked about his certain plays, my son would have limited information. He would say, "I hike the ball and hit my guy." In reality, my son saw less of the total action on the field than I had from the stands.

If you've ever watched a football game from the end zone and near ground level, you get a sense of how crazy and chaotic the game is. The ball is snapped, and big bodies fly everywhere. You wonder how the people on the field know what's going on with all the mass confusion occurring. The linemen—the guards, the tackles, the nose guard, and the center—see very little of the game. They focus on their assignment and the person they are supposed to block or tackle. When the ball is in play, they see very little of the other action.

Football coaches have learned the best perspective is far away from the action. The linemen do not call the plays and many times the quarterback does not even call the plays. The coach on the sideline makes decisions. Most times the decisions are made even further away in the press box. The best view of the game is from the press box. It sets high above the playing field, far enough back for coaches to see the whole field. Coaches even study film to build a historical perspective about the action on the field. They realize the importance of seeing the current realities: the strengths and weakness or their team and the opponent.

People with the vision to see things the way they really are have learned to "go to the press box" to create clarity of vision. They have learned the value of stepping back away from the confusion, action, and chaos of their own life to get a better perspective.

Objectivity

Another barrier to creating vision is objectivity. A computer software television commercial several years ago described a company working on a "can't miss" project, which somehow misses. The commercial says the software does not get flustered, does not get emotional, and does not fear change. The software analyzes the problem to arrive at a positive solution. The intended message of the advertising is to buy this software to help your company use the information it produces to make better business decisions. The more subtle message, however, involves objectivity and the usefulness of unbiased information in making rational decisions.

Emotional decisions are rarely wise decisions. Thinking emotionally and making assumptions based on how we feel at the moment clouds the true situation and restrict our ability to create a vision of the current reality.

One of Abraham Lincoln's many attributes during the American Civil War was his ability to be objective and not to be overly influenced by the crisis of the day. Lincoln served in a time of incredible confusion, political infighting, big egos, and swaying of public opinion.

Shelby Foote, an American Civil War writer and historian, talked about Lincoln's objectivity and was quoted in Ken Burn's film on the Civil War. *"A very mysterious man...he's got so many sides to him. The curious thing about Lincoln to me is that he could remove himself from himself as if he were looking at himself. It's a very strange, very eerie thing...and highly intelligent, a simple thing to say but (hard to do). Lincoln's been so smothered by stories of his compassion that people forget what a highly intelligent man he was...almost everything he did, almost everything, was calculated for effect."* This level of objectivity, to see situations from the "third person" perspective, is challenging but it increases the effectiveness of having a clear vision of the present.

One method to increase the ability to be more objective is to simplify the complicated. Taking situations and breaking them down to elements that are more fundamental helps remove the shroud of confusion, which becomes an obstruction to seeing the current reality. The purpose of the models or dynamics in this book are to help reduce the complexity of situations happening in life into workable information. This will help the reader understand the reality of the situation while planning for a favorable future.

Prejudice

People have a tremendous ability to rationalize behaviors. These rationalizations create an obstruction to clear vision and a barrier to success. Rationalizing is common for people to do but it is a dangerous activity when trying to create a clear and correct vision of the current reality. It leads to many vices and bad habits without the participant realizing the destructiveness of their behavior.

Prejudice, a preconceived judgment or opinion without having all the facts, is another barrier to creating vision. People have predetermined ideas based on previous experience or environment, which make it difficult to have vision for the current reality. Many times, people are prejudiced by past successes. Just because something or some circumstance has been true in the past does not mean it is reality in every situation. People emotionally tied to preconceived ideas, egos, and thoughts about their own virtues make it hard to face reality.

Paradigms and archetypes are words used to describe the barrier of preconceived ideas on objectively seeing the reality in situations and innovative solutions. Below is a simple demonstration to show the effect of prejudice and paradigms on vision. An anagram is a word made by transposing the letters of another word. For example: The letters INSTA could be changed to the word STAIN by rearranging the letters. Take a minute and determine the next several anagrams:

INTRA

ELCAM

THTRU

CKTRU

DSLEN

ONLEM

After deciphering these words, quickly decode the word on the following page:

A P C H E

Almost everyone will decipher CHEAP because the other words were solved by putting the first two letters of the anagram at the end of the word. Most people struggle decoding the first few words, but after the "system" has been established, they automatically use what has been successful. CHEAP is formed by using the paradigm and archetype used to spell TRAIN, CAMEL, TRUTH, TRUCK, LENDS and LEMON. APCHE, however, can also spell PEACH. Few people see this option because the preconceived idea about how to solve the puzzle has been quickly established. Human beings have the ability to develop habits quickly. This ability to establish archetypes can create a barrier to a clear and true vision of the current reality.

The Problem with Optical Illusions

Take a quick look at the simple optical illusions printed below.

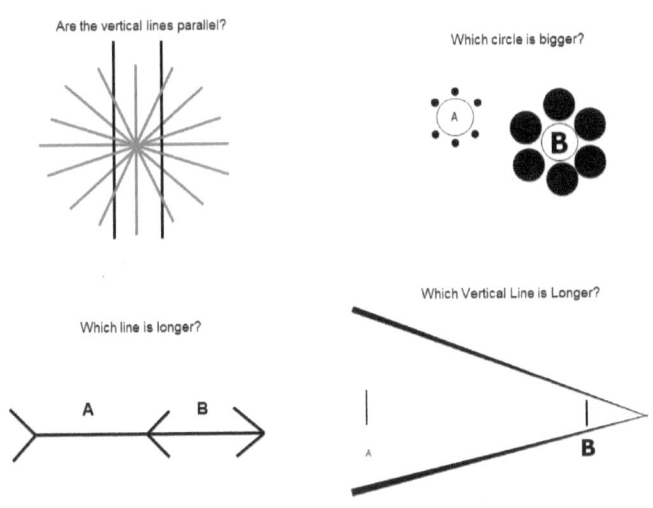

Do you think the three illusions that ask which is longer or bigger (A or B) are actually all the same? Most do.

Take a closer look at the last optical illusion.

Which Vertical Line is Longer?

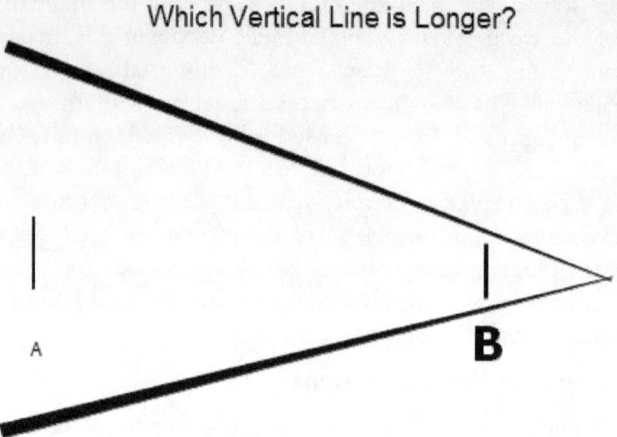

Here is the same illusion with the lines moved side-by-side.

Which Vertical Line is Longer?

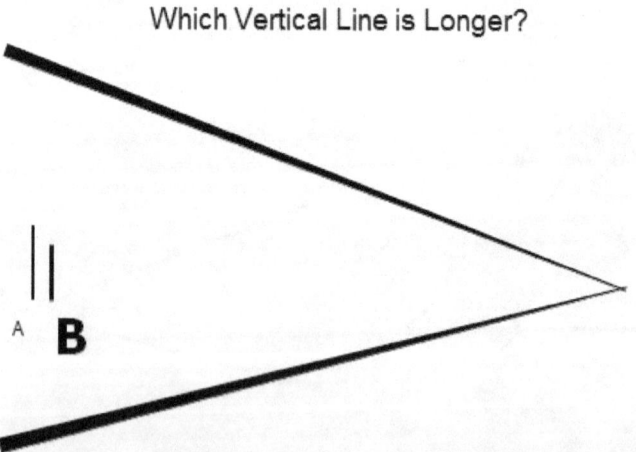

Most people quickly concluded the two lines in the last illusion were the same, although by simply measuring, you could determine line A is almost a third longer. Several factors deceive you in this simple illusion. The most obvious is the optical illusion itself. The angled lines, the different sized letters labeling the lines, and their distance from each other trick the eye. Each question about these illusions could be answered with the use of simple measuring device—a ruler.

Something else is at work in this exercise, however. Beyond the deceptive positioning of the lines, I easily created an archetype about how this activity works. All of the other optical illusions had objects the same size that looked different because of the confusing things around them. By the time we get to the last optical illusion, we know the lines are the same because we know it is a trick. We assume, although the lines are clearly not close to the same length, that the lines are the same. Our brains ignore that lines A and B actually look to be the same, which is a clear signal that something is different, because we have learned that making assumption saves us some time.

An illusion intellectually deceives or misleads. Many situations exists, which make seeing the current reality a challenge. Just as the surrounding in the optical illusions are diversions, preconceived ideas, irrelevant information, personalities, and surrounding circumstances are just a few distractions masquerading reality. In an optical illusion, we can know the truth, not by our own perspective or insight, but by developing way to measure what's actually happening. We need the same type of measurements to see the current reality in many interpersonal situations.

Magic, or the art of illusion, is based on a magician's ability to mask and deceive the eye. A skilled magician can make the impossible seem to happen right in front of your eyes. Simple optical illusions can also easily trick the eye and make distinguishing reality a challenge. Illusion become dangerous when we mistake them for the truth of a situation.

Accurately determining reality—to see the current situation— a person needs measurements on which they can rely. Working with any dynamic device requires knowing how to use the proper measuring instruments. A navigator uses a sextant, a meteorologist uses a barometer, a doctor may use an EKG, and a mechanical engineer uses a micrometer. To think dynamically and effectively work with people, a leader needs to develop methods to measure and

Seeing the current situation requires measurements

determine the current reality. Having a clear view of the present is a prerequisite to developing a view of the probable future.

THINKING YOU'RE GREAT KEEPS YOU FROM BEING GOOD

The management book *Good to Great* by Jim Collins, focuses on the differences between companies operating very well versus those at top financial performance. The major theme—"Good is the enemy of great." Millions have been inspired to improve their organizations by the premise of *Good to Great*. However, many groups struggle with thinking they are great, which prevents them from being even good! Ironically, the more insecure a group, the more they seem to live in a state of denial about current realities. Leaders need concrete measurements and definitions about success. They need to have the confidence to learn from mistakes and past experiences to develop excellence in themselves and their groups.

Humility (putting the needs of others first) requires the highest levels of self-assurance. Responsible leaders should be willing to challenge themselves and the group for future success. Living in the past or with the illusion your group is at the pinnacle of accomplishment is a sure path to demise. Illusions are dangerous because the cloak the current reality.

HOW TO CREATE A VISION OF THE CURRENT REALITY

Thinking dynamically does **not** require mystical or psychic abilities to foretell the future. It seeks to increase the ability to have a better vision of the present to create foresight for the future. There are some proven tools to help you develop your ability to create a view of the current reality.

Collect Data and Facts

Confusing opinion for truth is one of the primary barriers to having a clear view of the current reality and is a big source of interpersonal conflict. To create a vision of the current reality, a person needs to develop measurements and gather data for objective analysis. Admiral Grace Hopper, one of the innovators for the computer language COBAL once noted, "One accurate measurement is worth a thousand expert opinions."

Reflect

After gathering data and facts, try to reflect on the information to determine what it means. Data organized becomes information. Information when understood becomes knowledge. Knowledge when applied and used becomes and intelligence. Intelligence tempered with experience and reflection becomes wisdom.

Become as non-emotional as possible

Emotions are generally a poor basis for making decisions and emotion can certainly cloud the view of the current reality. Look for ways to remove yourself from situations. Try to "go to the press box" to gain perspective and objectivity.

Analyze the driving force and controlling force

One way to remove yourself from the haze that comes from being too emotionally involved in a situation is to look dynamically at situations by analyzing the driving forces and the controlling forces at work. This method allows you to see some of the underlying structures truly influencing events to let you understand them better.

Using the Power of Diversity

Diversity is an often overused word that is prevalent in attempts to get people to "get along" and "understand each other". What is sometimes missed is that getting perspective from individuals with different backgrounds, experiences, and points-of-view is extremely valuable in creating a vision for the current reality.

One classroom activity I often do with groups to demonstrate the importance of diverse perspectives and communication is to have them draw a picture of a penny. First they draw, based on memory all of the features of a penny. It is amazing how difficult it is to remember the details of something as common as a penny. After a few minutes, we will put the individuals into groups of four and have them repeat the exercise. Every time the group can come up with a better rendition of the penny than the individuals can working independently. Using the perspective of the group requires listening, respecting other points-of-view, and realizing that we rarely have all of the answers. The perspective of the group is a powerful tool in building a vision of the current reality.

Seeing the current reality is the foundation to thinking dynamically. The only effective way to foretell the future is to create your preferred future. The models in this book are tools to help you build that preferred future. Successful and effective people must have the vision to see reality, to create a positive tomorrow.

Key Points

- Having a vision for the future requires a clear vision of the present.
- Tomorrow is inherent in Today.
- "Go to the Press Box" to increase your perspective and objectivity of the present.
- Get perspectives from as many objective people as possible.
- Break complicated situations into simpler, more manageable information by a systematic approach.
- Try to see things from the "Third Person" perspective.
- Look for the driving forces and controlling forces in situations.
- Realize that finding truth is a challenging task, taking continuous effort with many barriers.

Chapter 3
Dynamic of Motivation:
Using the Natural Momentum of People's Needs to Influence a Group

"You will either step forward into growth or you will step back into safety."

Abraham Maslow

A variety of influences motivate people and groups. The specifics of the motivating force can vary greatly based on individual wants, needs, values, and desires. Two types of motivation generally categorize driving forces: fear and hope.

Fear is a strong motivator generating quick changes in behavior. I once worked with a man who smoked two packs of cigarettes a day for most of his life. Family, friends, and medical professionals all talked to him about the risk and tried to motivate him to stop. Nothing worked. The man often proclaimed, "I've tried to stop and simply can't." The habit was too strong and too addictive until the day he had a massive heart attack. He survived and the doctor explained his choices. He could continue to smoke and probably die in a few months or he could quit smoking and possibly live for many more years. The man quit.

Strongly influenced by the fear of death, he was able to break a habit he had been unable to change for nearly fifty years. He recovered, continued to work until retirement, and lived another 10 years. The last time I saw him, however, he had a pack of cigarettes in his pocket and had resumed his smoking habit. Fear, although a powerful motivator, is only effective as long as it is present. When the distress goes away, people tend to lose motivation and resume old habits.

Fear is effective in motivating people in the short-term, but often lacks the motivational force for long-term improvement and change. Fear is a negative motivational force. Fear motivates because people are avoiding something or are deprived of something. Groups relying on fear, coercive power, and intimidation will find this type of motivation has very little effect on people's long-term improvement.

Hope and aspiration influence the more positive aspects of motivation. This type of motivation may be more subtle to use and may take more time to see immediate movement, but motiving by hope and aspiration holds more promise for long-term learning and improvement.

Each year approximately 600,000 people have heart by-pass surgery and another 1.3 million have angioplasties. The root cause of these medical problems can often be traced to behavioral and lifestyle issues like diet, lack of exercise, smoking, alcohol, and stress. Many patients could avoid continued problems and pain by making constructive lifestyle changes. Almost all patients are given information about improving their lifestyle and many are told the consequences of continuing with their current habits. A recent medical study, however, showed that after two years 90% of the by-pass patients surveyed had not significantly changed their behavior. The fear motivating them for the first few months had failed to inspire lasting changes.

In 1993, the Mutual of Omaha insurance company did a study about the effects of lifestyle changes and motivation. They took 333 at-risk patients and put them into a program that included diet, exercise, and personal counseling. For one year, the group met two times a week for counseling and support services. One of the primary differences this group experienced compared to other self-help programs involved motivation. Typically, medical professionals had used fear and avoidance as the primary motivation for a person to change. In this test program, however, counselors focused on the more positive motivators of hope and aspiration. Counselors motivated patients by telling them they could feel better, not just live longer. They focused on the enjoyment of things that made daily life pleasurable. After three years, the study showed 77% of the participants had continued their positive lifestyle changes. Researchers concluded hope was a more powerful motivator than fear.

Goal setting, establishing purpose, and reminding people of the important things in life can be positive long-term motivators for continuous improvement.

Maslow's Hierarchy of Need

Abraham Maslow's theories of human motivation and his hierarchy of needs are frequently used to explain human behavior and the dynamics of why people act like they do. Maslow had a different perspective than most other research psychologist making his work particularly valuable in organizational development and understanding consumer behavior. His observations focused on individuals who were successful and well adjusted, instead of people with abnormalities or problems.

Maslow synthesized the thinking and research of many other psychologists to develop his premise of human motivation. Maslow wrote, "This theory is, I think, in the functionalist tradition of James and Dewey, and is fused with the holism of Wertheimer, Goldstein, and Gestalt psychology, and with the dynamicism of Freud, Fromm, Horney, Reich, Jung and Adler. This integration or synthesis may be called a holistic-dynamic theory."[2]

Maslow's Hierarchy of Needs

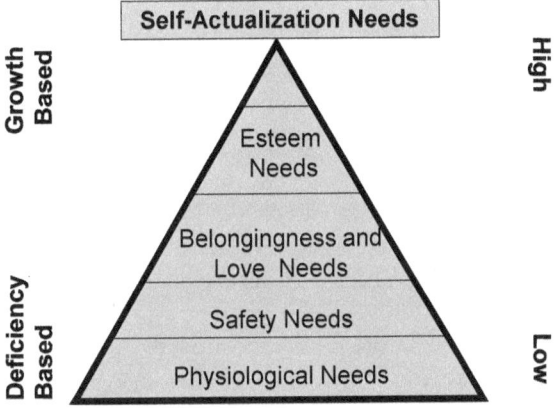

Maslow's theory says human needs are organized in a hierarchical structure. The lower needs must be met before the higher needs become motivating forces. The lowest and most basic needs are the *physiological needs*. A person must have the basic

---

[2] Maslow, Abraham H., *Motivation and Personality*, 2nd Edition, Harper and Row, 1970

biological needs like oxygen, hunger, thirst, and other bodily needs essential for survival satisfied before other needs become important. After physiological needs are met, the need for *safety* and *security* must be satisfied. The need for security, protection, avoidance of pain, avoidance of fear, and the need for order and structure in the environment are essential before a person can pursue higher order needs.

Hope and aspiration are the more positive aspects of motivation.

Both the physiological and safety needs are deficiency-oriented or fear-based; meaning a person only desires these things when they are absent. The other three levels of needs move toward what Maslow called meta-growth or growth motivation, which means the individual is moving toward a more enlightened experience of life.

After safety needs have been satisfied, the person will seek *belongingness* to a group. After the need for belongingness is fulfilled, the person likely pursues the desire for *esteem*, self-respect, and recognition. The highest level of need an individual can pursue is what Maslow and others call *self-actualization*. This state of being means self-fulfillment, independence, and enlightenment. Self-actualization was what Maslow observed in the most successful and well-adjusted individuals he studied.

The level of needs satisfaction in this hierarchy helps explain how and why people act in situations. For example, a person needs food to survive (Physiological). If there is a desperate need for food, people will do and eat almost anything to survive. Given a choice, however, they will choose clean, healthy food, which is appetizing (Safety). Most people do not like to eat alone so they invite a friend to eat at a restaurant (Belongingness/Love). They may want that friend to be impressed so they choose a fashionable restaurant with slightly higher prices and the right kind of clientele (Esteem). The self-actualized person will choose a dining experienced based not on what others think about them but based on what they appreciate. Desire is a powerful driving force in human motivation. Understanding how these forces are affecting you and how they affect others can help predict and influence future behaviors and reactions.

Individuals fulfilling deficiency-based needs, like physiological and safety needs, will be held more strongly by the force of status quo. **(See chapter 12, Dynamic of Change)** Those who are moving toward self-actualization will be more likely to exchange the confining forces of habit and fear with more enlightening and freeing forces like hope, exploration, and curiosity.

Organizational Hierarchy of Need

Groups of people also have hierarchy of needs motivating them. The first thing motivating a group is *survival*. They will search out leadership providing the best safety from layoffs, bankruptcy, changes, and other factors the group sees as a threat to their continued existence. An employee concerned with being fired or facing a plant closing is an example of someone likely to be motivated by survival. It will be difficult, if not impossible for that employee to look beyond the short-term situation to work creatively and successfully toward long-term goals.

After the need for survival is met and the individual no longer fears their immediate demise, groups will look for security. The

Dynamic of Organizational Hierarchy of Needs

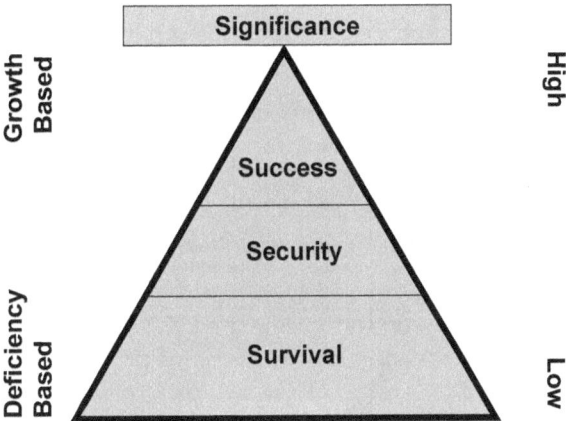

employee might desire affirmations from the employer about their role in an organization or seek job benefits that will help secure their longevity. Only after an environment is established where members feel safe and secure, can a group strive for the next level, the desire for success. Groups looking for motivation beyond success will seek significance or the ability to make a difference.

DEVELOPING A GROUP

Leading people through the organizational hierarchy of needs involves a certain amount of conflict management **(See Chapter 10, Dynamic of Conflict)**. Successful leaders need to analyze the performance/maturity level in their group and determine the conflict/stress level in designing effective motivational strategies. The graphic below shows the relationship between conflict/stress and performance/maturity within an organization. Motivational needs or the group change based on these factors. Moving groups through these various phases of performance and conflict require a leader to use a variety of motivational strategies.

Conflict/Stress and Performance/Maturity with the Organizational Hierarchy of Needs

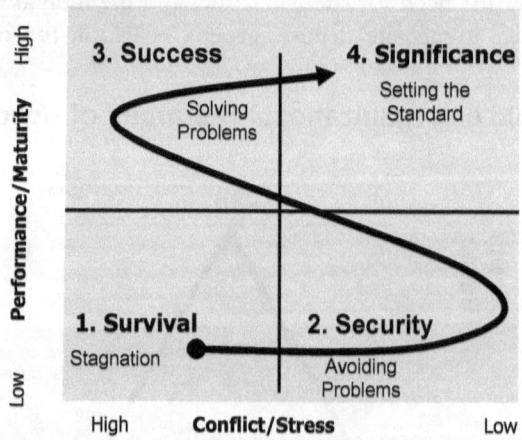

Groups in the survival quadrant of this chart typically have high levels of stress and very low levels of performance, because almost all of their energies focus on their continued existence. Moving a group from survival to security requires a reduction in the stress or conflict in the organization. In the security mode, groups will sense a reduction in the stress level, but the performance may remain low.

Ironically, as a group moves from security to success, they will probably experience increased stress and conflict as they improve performance. In fact, a leader may need to subject a group that is comfortable in the security quadrant to some level of conflict to induce learning, positive adaptation, and change. The added stress, if it is not critical, can act as a driving force for positive change. Those groups who can achieve significance (groups that are aligned with and achieving their mission) will be the highest in maturity and performance as well as having less stress and conflict in the organization.

SURVIVAL

Groups in the survival quadrant will have low performance/maturity and high levels of conflict/stress. These groups stagnate and become paralyzed with inactivity. They have a difficult time seeing past the crisis of the moment and will often be in denial of their poor performance. These groups typically have not developed the ability to take responsibility for their actions.

Things To Do:

A common mistake for a leader is to challenge this group with lofty goals and ideals. Groups in the survival quadrant do not have the capacity to accept these challenges. The capability for success must be developed. The first step in developing capability for success is to provide safety and security for the group by clearly setting parameters for behavior and defining the tolerance for failure with written policies and procedures. Directives need to be clear and concise to lessen the chaos of the situation. Set realistic and even simplified goals and reward the smallest of successes. Eliminate the "rumor mill" by providing information, feedback, reinforcement, and correction quickly and clearly. Get this group to deal in data and facts instead of opinion and innuendo. This group will need to be taught responsibility.

Leadership Strategies: Lead by directing, protecting, and parenting.

SECURITY

Before a group can achieve success, a leader must provide a sense of safety and security. Lower levels of conflict/stress and low levels of performance/maturity characterize groups in the security quadrant. Groups moving from survival to security will want to avoid mistakes and problems. This is a comfortable situation for a group to be in so the big challenge is to get them to a higher performance level.

Things To Do:

A leader will need to teach this group problem solving skills and give them permission to make mistakes within a limit of tolerance. This group will need to have the measurements of success well defined. The challenge is to move a group from this low stress, low conflict environment into a more high performance and challenging environment that may produce some constructive stress.

Leadership Strategies: Lead by coaching and teaching the group about expectations for success and the parameters or limits for failure.

SUCCESS

Groups motivated by success will have higher levels of performance/maturity but may also have higher levels of conflict/stress as they grow and learn new skills and tackle greater challenges. This can be a very rewarding quadrant, but conflict management skills are needed. These groups will need to learn to accept responsibility for mistakes and treat problems as opportunities.

Things To Do:

Define success and purpose for the group. They will be motivated by reward and recognition. Encourage independent initiative and teach some conflict resolution skills. The goal of a leader with a group functioning at this level is to prepare them for the highest organizational level...doing significant things.

Leadership Strategies: Leaders should challenge and develop individuals in the group.

SIGNIFICANCE

These are very rare groups, which are able to function at the highest levels or organizational excellence. Setting the standard and learning from mistakes motivates these high functioning groups.

Things To Do:

This group will need little direction, so a leader can focus on establishing and defining purpose for the group as well as helping create a vision of the current reality and designing a preferable future.

Leadership Strategies: Leaders dealing with these rare groups can focus on developing future leaders.

Survival, security, success, and significance are levels of performance requiring various motivation strategies. Effective leaders have the vision to see the level their group is functioning at to make adjustments and set the framework for motivation to the next highest level.

Importance of Momentum within a Group

Throughout most of humankind's history, travel by water has been the most efficient mode of transportation. Great ships could be constructed carrying large cargos. The driving forces, like wind, men rowing, and later engines could easily move a boat through the less resistant force of the water. A ship, however, is difficult if not impossible to steer, if it doesn't have forward momentum. Without adequate driving force, the ship will drift, controlled by unpredictable outside forces, instead of being guided by the controlling force of the rudder.

Organizations are much like a ship on the water; they need forward momentum before they can be effectively guided. Groups need to be influenced, but the effective leader must be able to determine the driving and controlling forces to achieve positive outcomes.

I was once involved with a group doing strategic planning and working through a period of turmoil and change. The strengths (which in strategic planning are often exaggerated) and the weaknesses (which in strategic planning are generally understated) were listed and the comment was made, "This organization is like a nuclear powered submarine; that's being rowed...and some of the people are rowing the wrong direction!" The person felt the organization had a lot of potential, like the technically advanced submarine, but the potential was not being realized because they were stagnating. Not only was the potential not being realized, the members of the group were not even clear about the direction they should try to go.

Leading an organization with no forward momentum is about as easy as trying to row a submarine. An ocean-going vessel relies on its forward momentum for steering, and organizations rely on momentum for direction. Stagnant organizations must have leadership creating movement, motivation, and driving forces.

One way to create momentum in an organization is to "move downhill" by letting the organization begin movement in the easiest direction (even if it is not the preferred direction) to generate enough momentum to be turned. Sometimes this is the only way to get a group moving. Leading an organization is sometimes more like driving a battleship than a speedboat; change comes gradually and in proportion to the size and momentum of the organization.

For example, a new manager goes into a department, which is demoralized with a reputation for low performance. The manager can give motivational speeches, throw tirades, and maybe even throw a few chairs, but the stagnate inertia of the group makes it impossible to positively affect the attitude and morale of the group. The manager has to get the group moving—focused on a purpose.

The planning dynamic **(See Chapter 8, Dynamic of Planning)** can be a strong tool for creating this type of driving force. One effective strategy in creating forward momentum is to set realistic and very obtainable initial goals for the group, then celebrate the accomplishments, no matter how small. These goals do not have to be earth shattering or the long-term objectives for the organization. The goals may even be in a slightly different direction than the long-term objectives, but by celebrating the accomplishments and generating excitement, the leader creates momentum they can use to guide the group to better objectives.

Another way to get a group moving is to start small in building momentum. One mistake many organizations make is having too many meetings and discussions before generating momentum for an idea. This often gives too many people the opportunity to distract and derail the driving force, thus avoiding change and positive improvement. Participatory leadership, getting the view from as many people as possible and involving all people in the organization to implement goals is vital, however, generating momentum and getting the organization moving is better done with a few, dedicated individuals who are willing to do the work of starting.

One of the most successful change events I ever witnessed started with a small nucleus of people who were able to build momentum for the whole group. This new and innovative idea had not been tried before and this organization had been in a period of conflict and low morale. This organization was stagnated by negative attitudes and people protecting their turf in a survival mode of motivation. Often when trying something new, the force of the status quo freezes new ideas. The planning for this project started with three individuals until the concept built momentum. People were brought into the project as needed until a critical mass of excitement and support developed for the project. Timing was critical. No one wants to be left out, and people feeling excluded will become a force of resistance. By the time the idea was brought to the whole group, there was a bandwagon of enthusiasm making it difficult for even the most cynical members of the group to cause much resistance.

Once an organization is put into motion, it must be directed. Leadership must understand the forces affecting organizations and attempt to control these forces to direct the group. Leaders must be able to create movement toward positive activities by employing the appropriate driving forces while influencing the group's direction with the suitable controlling forces.

Underlying Structures

Ability in predicting the results of various forces on individuals and situations comes from understanding the dynamic of force and underlying structures controlling them. The momentum of physical objects tend to go where there is the least resistance. Groups also follow the course of least resistance.

The force of gravity is pulling everything to the lowest level of solid ground. Rain falling on a continental divide begins moving downhill. The final destination of the water can be altered by hundreds of miles depending on the side of the mountain on which the water falls. If a person would step back and study the terrain, an accurate prediction could be made about the path of the water based on the topography and other factors like the hardness or softness of the rock over which the water is flowing. The predictions might not be absolutely correct, but the general flow of the water could be understood. Likewise, leaders who take the time to create a vision of the current reality are analyzing the personalities, the morale, and the maturity of the group as well as a host of other underlying structures affecting the actions and performance.

Underlying structures influence the intensity and magnitude of a force. These controlling influences affect the direction of the force. Flying over the United States is a routine experience for many people. A trip across the country is comprised of a nap, a bag of snacks, a drink, and maybe some reading. Few experienced passengers spend much time looking out of the window. I am much the same way but there are a few natural wonders I will take the time to try to see from the air—the Grand Canyon, the Rocky Mountains, and the mighty Mississippi River.

The Mississippi River is one of the few natural features easily seen and distinguished from 30,000 feet. When viewing this river from the sky, it looks like a giant snake winding its way toward the Gulf of Mexico. Along both sides of the river, you can see what looks like crescents carved in the adjacent fields. These crescents are where the river used to flow. The Mississippi River, like any body of water, is fluid and moving. The water is being pulled by the driving force of gravity toward the ocean, but the controlling force of the riverbank can be changed or broken based on the underlying structure.

There is a permanent battle between the U.S. Army Corp of Engineers and the Mississippi River. The Corp of Engineers attempts to control the force, the direction, and the economic value of the river by controlling its underlying structure. In 1837, the changing course of the Mississippi River threatened the booming frontier city of St. Louis. A new officer and army engineer, Robert E. Lee, was dispatched to work on the problem. The city's harbor was in danger of being blocked by two islands being created by the flow and force of the water. The main channel of the river moved toward the Illinois side and away from the excellent harbor at St. Louis. The Illinois side was flatland not desirable for docking boats.

Dredging activities had been expensive and with the technology of the day, not very successful. The force of the river was greater than the efforts to control it. Lee's solution was to work with the force of the river by changing the underlying structure. A dike was built a few miles upstream on the Illinois side diverting the channel back toward St. Louis. The sand islands threatening the harbor did not have to be moved my manmade machines. Controlling the water flow, changing the underlying structure, meant the river itself would destroy the islands and return the channel to the safe harbor of St. Louis.[3] As an engineer, Lee understood the driving force gravity had on the water and how to manipulate the controlling force of the riverbank to alter the underlying structure.

Effective leaders also know how to work with existing forces and change the behavior of people by changing the underlying structure. It is hard to tell people what to do. They naturally resist change, even when the change is beneficial. It is easier to give people choices explaining to them the consequences and rewards for their actions and work with the existing structure.

Working in sales, you learn it is easier to let people choose than trying to tell them what to do. In sales, you have no alternative since the customer is trading their money for their satisfaction. Selling is a matter of finding the motivators (what the customer wants from the product) and overcoming objections. You work with the motivation of the customer combined with what you have to offer. Effective sales people know how to manipulate the underlying structure to match their product to the customer's desires.

Leaders may use the different personalities, the strengths, or even the weaknesses of individuals in a group to achieve results. Putting the right people in the right situation is one method leaders can use to work with the underlying structure to move the group in a desirable direction.

Understanding the underlying structure of situations as well as the scope and effect of the forces involved can help in decision-making and influencing events. Working against these forces can be frustrating, ineffective, and even destructive. People and situations are affected by these forces all of the time. Learning to recognize and understand driving and controlling forces is a beginning to understanding the many dynamics influencing situations.

---

[3] Freeman, Douglas, S., R.E. Lee A Biography, 1950, Charles Scribner's Sons, New York

Leaders Role in Understanding Force

Invisible social and psychological forces affect how people act and react. Organizations depend on the force of momentum for direction. Groups of people are generally moving in one direction or the other. Maintaining positive momentum and altering motion going in the wrong direction requires vision and leadership. Driving forces must be balanced with controlling forces.

Groupthink and the culture of a group can be a strong and pervasive influence, greatly affecting the attitude and morale of an organization. Although change in inevitable, most groups and individuals are affected by the force of the status quo, which resist the needed changes. The forces of fear and habit are two factors strengthening the force of the status quo. The force of desire and the vision to see the need to change help break the force of the status quo. Finally, the underlying structure is what guides, directs, and affects any force. To work effectively with the social forces at work, these underlying structures must be understood and constructed to use the strength of these forces.

Key Points

- Driving force and controlling force must be in balance for an organization to accomplish goals.
- Without adequate driving force, it is often difficult to use controlling force in an organization.
- Leaders need to understand the underlying structure influencing situations and look for ways to manipulate the underlying structure for controlling force.

Chapter 4
Dynamic of Influence:
Using Influence and Vision to
Provide Force and Direction for a Group

Vision provides controlling force—influence the driving force.

Football is an exciting game to watch. Players, teams, rivalries, marching bands, referees, the stadium, hot dogs, and a variety of beverages are all part of the show. Of course, no game would be complete without cheerleaders. These spirited young men and women jump, yell, tumble, and defy gravity with acrobatic feats to inspire the crowd to cheer. They are after all cheer "LEADERS." Cheerleaders have a vital role in controlling and influencing a crowd, but like many other leaders, they are leaders in name and title only. Like other leaders, they have limited influence over the crowd. If things are going badly for the home team, they have little effect in making the crowd cheer.

The same crowd, however, which has been disinterested in responding to the cheerleaders' repeated request to cheer, will sometimes come to life at certain points of the game. They will often stand and shout in unison, as if directed by an all-powerful force. The crowd will yell, scream, groan, or gasp with the unique sound of a crowd at a sporting event. They will react, not because of the cheerleaders and their efforts to support the team, but by **the action on the field.** The very game, which brought the crowd to the stadium, motivates them to cheer. A first down, a long run, a good tackle, a touchdown, the action on the field will lead, influence, and dictate the morale of the crowd more than the cheerleaders will!

What happens to cheerleaders at a football game is not significantly different from what happens to other leaders. Often the efforts of the leader are not as influential as other external factors. Leadership, many times, does not require yelling and screaming to get action as much as it relies on paying attention to the action on the field and those powerful external forces motivating the group to cheer, to fear, or to be apathetic. Leadership requires vision and influence.

BUILDING BLOCKS OF INFLUENCE

Fundamental building blocks of influence include competence, attitude, trust, and relationships.

Building Blocks of Influence

Competence

The foundation of influence is **competence** or the ability to achieve. Competence or "expert power" often depends on the reputation a leader has in achieving or failing. Leading by competence only goes as far as the leader's successes. When a leader is perceived as incompetent, they lose influence quickly with the group, since there is little emotional tie to this type of leadership. Motivational needs for safety, security, camaraderie, and recognition drive people within a group. Groups predominately influenced by the level of competence or expertise will gravitate toward the person best supplying these needs.

Competence is essential in building influence. Three methods to build influence through competence include:

1. **Consistently doing the right things**
2. **Exceeding expectations**
3. **Solving problems**

A person's abilities, skill level, and aptitude determine their competence. Consistently **doing the right thing,** builds a person's perceived expertise with others. Building competence is like playing poker. The more success you have, the more risk you can take. People with a reputation for being competent can make more mistakes and have more learning experiences than a person without the same perceived level of competence. The perception of competence is important in building leadership influence.

Another effective method to build competence is to exceed expectations. **Setting realistic expectations is one of the best tools to improve perceived competence and build influence.** I have often witnessed people in organizations accomplishing some level of success, but they have set such high levels of expectations, that the success has limited impact. A salesperson who over-promises a product's capability, a service technician who consistently is late for appointments, or a manager who promises more results than can be achieve are examples of not meeting expectations and thus eroding the perceived level of competence. On the other hand, I have seen individuals leverage their natural abilities into greater perceive competence by consistently exceeding expectations. Knowing expectations and consistently exceeding those expectations is a powerful method to improve influence through competence.

Problem solving abilities is another way leaders demonstrate competence. **(See Chapter 9, Dynamic of Problem Solving)** Problem solving and managing conflict involves having a clear vision of the current reality, innovative thinking, and the ability to have a learning attitude. Providing safety and security to a group by solving problems is a sure technique to build influence by showing competence.

Attitude

Leaders reflect the **attitude** of the group and the attitude of the group often reflects the leader's attitude. A leader's personal attitude is important, but the way his or her attitude affects the group is of greater consequence.

Leaders have many responsibilities but one of the most important is how their attitude affects followers. Attitude reflects leadership, because leaders are responsible for the attitude and morale of the group. Leaders must be aware of their non-verbal messages. Their countenance has a powerful effect on others. The need for safety and assurance motivates people. Followers depend on leaders who give them confidence. Effective leaders know the power of reflecting attitudes that positively influence the group's morale.

Winston Churchill, British Prime Minister during World War II, was a sterling example of leadership under duress. He demonstrated the importance of reflecting a positive attitude. Churchill knew as well as any person in his country that the war situation was desperate in England during the early years of the war. He knew his small, island nation faced invasion and possibly defeat. Churchill's demeanor and attitude during the dark years of 1939 and 1940 were unmistakably optimistic, at least in his public speeches and appearances. Churchill once said, "A pessimist sees the difficulty in every opportunity, an optimist sees the opportunity in every difficulty." This reflection of a positive attitude increased Churchill's influence and ability to lead in a time of crisis.

Demonstrating optimistic or positive attitudes is a strong driving force. People can be influenced by fear and avoidance or by aspirations, goals, and purpose. Leading by coercion has a limited capacity for long term influence while **helping people dream, achieve goals, and feel significant in fulfilling their purpose has almost unlimited scope for lasting influence.** Extraordinary leaders know how to use the perception of attitude to build influence within the group. Leaders must often have the courage to be positive even when faced with great challenges.

Trust

One of the most important elements in creating enduring influence is **trust**. It is a commodity earned gradually over time. A leader's aptitude to influence at any level depends on his or her ability to develop trust among the group. Having trust in a leader takes an emotional commitment from the follower.

Building trust is much like starting a small business. A business can start with meager resources and little cash. Few mistakes can be made and the businessperson will need to manage well to survive. As the business prospers and the bank account swells, the businessperson can take more chances in decision-making based on the increased wealth of the business. One mistake may not mean certain ruin like it did in the beginning. However, if the businessperson makes reckless decisions that lose money, he or she may return to the same situation with little money and little room to make mistakes in managing the business.

Leaders build trust as a businessperson builds a bank account—based on past performance and performance over time. The businessperson can squander the bank account with poor business choices and leaders can use up their trust with the group by mismanaging that trust. Trust is like a tube of toothpaste, much easier to squeeze out than to put back in. Using up the trust people have in you is easy, but building it back is difficult to impossible. Building trust takes time and commitment but can be expended very quickly. A leader can build the level of trust people have in them by being reliable, consistent, honest, and credible.

Relationships

Competence begins the process of building influence. Trust and attitude add to this foundation of influence. The most powerful component of influence, however, is the ability to build **relationships**—people following because they want to. Building organizations depend on developing and building up people in the organization. Being a leader takes courage and requires a person to not only take responsibility for his or her actions, but also for the development and welfare of the group.

Building influence by constructing relationships is the most enduring and the most powerful level of influence. It is also the hardest level of influence to master. This type of influence challenges leaders to develop people to their highest potential. Motivating and developing other people results in a multiplier effect on group performance.

One of the biggest challenges in supervision and management is the inability to replicate talent. People who were good, productive workers with expertise in a specific job are often promoted to supervisor positions with little training in supervision and management. These production experts often solve problems by jumping in and doing the work. This may be a short-term remedy, but unless they are able to train other workers to work at their high level, they will fail at the job of supervision. Delegating, empowering, and encouraging are difficult work, but they are essential elements in developing people and replicating expertise.

Good leaders want better people around them. When leaders attempt to make others better than themselves, they prove they are worthy to be a leader. Building relationships and replicating talent, however, requires more than just having a positive attitude, being affable to other people, and encouraging them. Developing people involves learning and often learning includes stress and discomfort. Teaching people to be responsible and preparing them to take authority for decisions can means stress, conflict, and chaos for a group. **(See Chapter 11, Dynamic of Authority and Responsibility)**

Building influence by building relationships is not easy. It takes a genuine interest in people along with high self-assurance, which allows the leader to put the needs of others before their own needs. The highest levels of self-assurance are found in the humility of those rare people living the golden rule— ***"Treat others the way you want to be treated."*** Great leaders are in the people-development and people-encouragement business. Their tremendous influence is founded on trust, attitude, and competence, but is multiplied by their ability to build relationships. Leaders who excel at developing people in an organization do so by empowering and preparing them instead of directing and controlling them. They prepare people to succeed, make sure they have the tools and resources needed, and then allow people to do their best work.

HIERARCHY OF LEADERSHIP

Position

Leadership and influence have escalating levels of effectiveness. The lowest level of leadership is leadership by **position**. People designated as "the Boss" have a certain amount of leadership authority by virtue of their job title and position. Leadership by position alone, however, comes with little real influence. Leadership by position is based on *coercive* power or *reward* power, the ability to supply compensation. The ability of the leader to punish or reward may be the only power these leaders have with the group. A position or title is given while influence must be earned. Many times the real leaders in a group are not the positional leader. Real leaders will be the ones with the highest level of influence over people. This influence can be positive or negative, constructive or destructive.

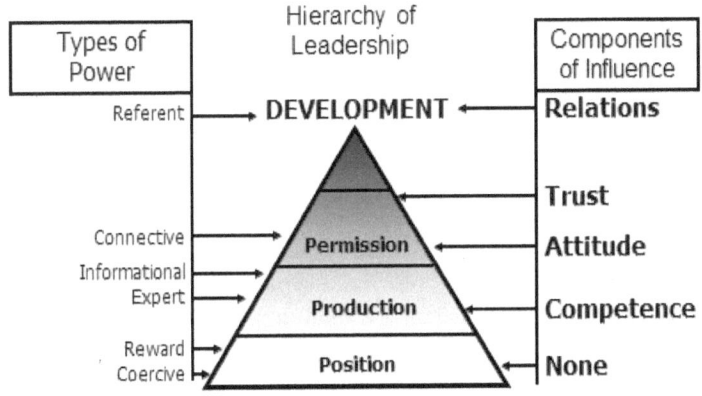

During the American Civil War, women were not allowed to serve in the military or hold any official position in the war effort. However, one northern journalist wrote, "No conflict in history was so much a woman's war as the civil war." Poor sanitary conditions and the great loss of life due to disease caused the formation of the Sanitary Commission in the North. Many women, Union and Confederate, were involved in nursing and caring for the condition of the men. One Quaker widow, Mary Ann Bickerdike, traveled with the Union army four years and through 19 battles. She assisted in amputations, brewed coffee, and secured food to feed the men. The men called her Mother Bickerdike and by the end of the war, General William Tecumseh Sherman said simply, "She ranks me."[4] Having the title of leader is not the same as being a leader. True leadership comes by influence.

A young lieutenant stationed for his first tour of duty in Vietnam was frustrated because the men seemed to be influenced

---

[4] The Civil War, Florentine Films, Ken Burns

more by the sergeant of the platoon during battle than by his orders. The men had experience with the sergeant and knew he had been able to keep them alive in the past. Survival is a powerful influencer. The lieutenant found the men were often reluctant to follow his orders without the approval of the sergeant. The lieutenant discovered that until he had proved himself in battle and earned the trust of the men, he would not be as influential as the sergeant. Rank, he was told, is something you wear—respect must be earned. Leading by position, without influence, is a weak leadership position. People follow when they have to, but when the battle starts they will be looking around to see who is really in charge.

Production

The next level of influence, **production,** involves the ability of a leader to produce results. People achieving results obtain a higher level of influence than people leading purely by position. Group achievement and leading by production will cause groups and individuals to have higher morale. When things get done and goals are met, there is a sense of accomplishment and success. Informational power and expertise can increase this type of leadership. Competence (the ability to achieve) is necessary to lead by production or results. People with a proven record of accomplishment and success possess higher levels of influence.

Permission

The third level of influence is leading by **permission**. This is an enviable leadership role because people are now following because they want to. Leadership by permission means people have confidence in the leader. These leaders have the personal charisma and people skills to get others on their side. Leadership by permission is slightly more effective than leading by production but generally will occur only after a leader has demonstrated competence. Leaders with high levels of performance can sometimes have greater influence than leaders who are well liked.

Trust is essential for leading by permission. For a person to follow a leader by choice, the person must have strong confidence in that leader. People who are trusted always have tremendous influence regardless of their rank or position. Effective leaders develop strategies to increase their ability to lead by production and by permission. Leaders who are able to lead by permission generally have the ability to connect with the followers or are perceived to have connective power to other people that can help the group achieve survival, security, or success.

The most effective leaders will be those understanding the importance and responsibility of leadership in developing others in the group. Leaders combining the influence of production with the influence of permission are leading in a highly effective manner. Leading by production and permission is also a prerequisite to leading with the highest level of influence...leadership by development.

Development

The highest level of leadership involves people **development**. At this level of leadership, the organization is growing in a multiplying fashion. Leaders at this level are preparing others to lead. Leaders with this ability have the highest levels of growth, loyalty, success, and satisfaction. They establish trust, reflect a positive attitude, demonstrate competence to lead, and build effective relationships with people and groups.

The highest level of leadership and influence is the ability to develop the talents of others around you. The ability to develop relationships and to communicate ideas is a sure way to bring out the best in your leadership potential. Leading by development, encouraging, and building people up, multiplies influence and leadership.

Example of Team Building and the Hierarchy of Leadership

The following example is based on a team building exercise used involving golf equipment. This activity shows how leadership works in a very practical application. Since we cannot go to the golf course, we will imagine how this scenario might work with your co-workers or friends and how it might apply to your leadership situation.

This team building game uses shortened golf holes (usually 100 to 150 yards from the target) and a variety of balls including soft rubber balls, tennis balls, super balls, and real golf balls. Each team consist of four players who are given a pitching wedge, a 9-iron, an 8-iron, and a 7-iron to play with. (Each type of ball and club has a different characteristic.) Players use the equipment assigned to them during the playing of a hole and they can trade equipment at the end of each hole. A "leader" is randomly picked to make the decisions about the assignment of equipment and the order of play for their team.

Stage One

To begin the activity, each team member is given a club to use and a ball by the leader. Each individual plays their ball and counts up the number of strokes they use until the ball is in the hole. A typical team will have members with varying experience, expertise, and aptitude in playing golf. The team with the combined lowest amount of strokes wins the hole and gets points. In addition, the individual with the lowest stroke total for each team gets additional individual points.

Stage Two

The team selects a new team leader after the first stage. What happens in the leadership dynamic is predictable. The best and most talented player, the person with the most competence, generally takes over the responsibilities of leadership from the person that was assigned to be the positional leader. For the next two holes, each person hits a shot and after all the players hit, the team chooses the best shot to play next. (In golf, this is commonly called a scramble.) All players then play from place where the best shot ended. The best player will typically get the best club, the best ball, and be in charge of the team's success. Weaker players are often ignored while everyone focuses on helping the leader achieve.

Stage Three

The rules or controlling force change for each stage of the activity. In stage three, the captain assigns the equipment and balls like in the previous holes. However, for these next two holes, once a player's shot is used, that player cannot play again until all members of the team have contributed at least one shot. The decision-making changes dramatically, because the team can no longer rely solely on one person with expertise to accomplish team goals. Suddenly the team may decide to use a weaker player's shot to save the better player's skill for more challenging situations. At the end of the stage, the team is asked to vote for the most valuable player. Sometimes the most skilled or competent player is chosen, but often the player who performs above expectations or the most improved player is chosen as the most valuable.

Stage Four

In stage four, the captain still assigns equipment and makes decisions about the sequence of play, but in this round the team must play the worst shot that the team hits. Suddenly the role of leadership changes again. The skill and ability of the best player is negated and the ability to teach and develop the weaker players is valued. After the end of these two holes, the team is asked to select the most valuable player. The person chosen is always someone who is encouraging and able to teach and improve the other players. The competence needed is not the ability to play, but the ability to develop all of the players

Stage Five

For the final hole, players go back and play by the rules of stage one. Everyone hits his or her own shot while keeping a combined score. Invariably the team's score and performance improves. Leadership evolves from:

- **(Positional)** someone being assigned as leader to,
- **(Production)** someone assuming leadership by her or his skill, ability, and competence to,
- **(Permission)** leaders chosen because their attitudes encourage and build trust with others to
- **(Development)** leaders who are best able to develop the other people around them to be better.

Using the components of influence (competence, attitude, trust, and relationships) to work through the hierarchy of leadership (position, production, permission, and development) is an effective method to develop teams that achieve, succeed, and accomplish more as group than they can as individuals.

Fluency of Leadership

Highly effective leaders have an aptitude and ability to clearly see the reality of a situation and naturally use the dynamics at work to get things done. They are able to change and move with these dynamics to influence behavior, morale, and the attitude of others.

Fluency in leadership is comparable to obtaining fluency in a second language. Learning a second language happens in stages. First, some cognitive information must be learned. What are the letters? How are words and sentences formed? Next, the learner will make associations to things they already know. Some words in the new language may sound like words in the old language. At this stage, the learner will struggle and be awkward in their speech. Later in the learning process, the learner will become more comfortable with the new skill. They may become fluent in the second language, which means they will be able to communicate without thinking about the techniques of the new language. They will be able to get their ideas across smoothly and naturally without thinking about the new language.

The most effective leaders are fluent in using the dynamics of interpersonal relationships to build influence. They are able to see the situation clearly and adapt in order to get positive results. Leaders who are expert at understanding the forces at work in groups may often seem as if they are doing very little. Their fluency in understanding and influencing situations, like a person fluently speaking a second language, is natural and effortless.

> **The most effective leaders are fluent in using the dynamics of interpersonal relationships to build influence.**

Some people are natural leaders, which mean they have an aptitude and fluency in understanding influence, vision, communication, and the dynamic forces in situations. Understanding the dynamics of leadership and interpersonal relationships is instinctive to them. Others can learn the dynamics of leadership by knowing, understanding, and using driving force and controlling force until they gain fluency and become leaders with influence.

Leadership requires influence and vision. It also requires the leader to take responsibility for the morale and achievement of the group. The job of a leader is not always to tell people where to go or what to do. A leader's job is to create a vision for the group by seeing the needs, challenges, and current realities of the group while using the influence of leadership to guide the group to the preferable future.

A leader must define the purpose and mission of the group. They can use purpose, mission, and other motivators to create driving force. Leaders will also need to manipulate the important controlling or constraining forces to maximize influence. The leader's role is to identify the purpose of the group and focus the group's attention on that purpose. Leaders not only deal with the current situation of the group, they must be able to determine future challenges and prepare the group to make positive changes to deal with the ever-changing challenges. Leaders not only lead for today but also for tomorrow.

Key Points

- Leadership is not merely a position it is influence.
- The components of influence include:
  o Competence
  o Attitude
  o Trust
  o Relationships
- Build influence through competence by
  o Consistently doing the right things,
  o Exceeding expectations and,
  o Solving problems
- The levels of leadership influence include
  o Positional authority
  o Production or achieve results through competence
  o Permission where people are leading because the trust a leader and like their attitude
  o Development leadership when leaders are developing the people around them to function at the highest levels.
- Trust is built slowly over time but can be lost in an instant of poor judgment.
- Attitude of the group often reflects the attitude of leadership.

Bob Perry

Chapter 5
Dynamic of Groupthink:
Overcoming Peer Pressure and
Negative Attitudes in Groups

*"The secret of managing is to keep the guys who hate you
away from the guys who are undecided."*

Casey Stengel

The mind is a powerful thing. A person's success depends in part on their capacity to develop a positive self-image and a belief in their abilities. Self-talk or affirmation is a term psychologists use to describe how a person views their abilities, value, and worth.

Self-talk is a powerful force in influencing a person's behavior, but it is often overwhelmed by the phenomenon of "groupthink." Solomon E. Asch, a social psychologist, conducted experiments with groups of people showing the effects of conformity and peer pressure. The experiment involved one test subject who was placed in a group with six other individuals who were confederates of the experimenter. The subject was told they were being tested for visual judgment. They were shown one vertical line and asked to match the line with one of three other lines, which would be the same length. The answers were given aloud and for the first few rounds, all of the individuals gave the correct answer.

Later, the individuals working for the experimenter would give wrong answers to see what response the test subject would be. After hearing the other "peers" give the wrong answer, the test subjects overwhelmingly agreed with the majority...even though the right answers to the test were obvious. Only 29% of the subjects tested never yielded to the bogus majority. [5] This study on group conformity demonstrates the powerful effect groups have on individual thinking and inherent need to fit in to a group.

---

[5] Asch, S. E., (1956). Studies of Independence and Conformity: I. A Minority of One Against a Unanimous Majority. Psychological Monographs, 70 (Whole N. 416)

Many outside influences are at work in groups of people causing those groups to move in a direction. The values, beliefs, and attitudes of an individual affects their decisions, but the force of the group can be an even bigger influence. The force causing an individual's thinking to conform to the group beliefs is groupthink.

People often have a "herd" mentality. We perceive safety in numbers and feel comfortable when we are conforming to group norms, even when the group norms are destructive.

Adolph Hitler's Nazi Germany participated in destructive groupthink. Hitler's henchmen were masters at understanding the power and influence of groupthink. By creating a critical mass of thought, they were able to get a whole nation to do things, which would have been unthinkable to an objective, rational thinking individual. People have a tremendous ability to rationalize actions and falsehoods. One of the most powerful rationalizations is the idea that if everyone is thinking or acting a certain way, it must be the right way. This group morality is a dangerous and provocative factor. As Solomon wrote, "There is a way which seems right to a man, but its end leads to destruction."

Gravity is a physical force pervading the whole universe. Gravitation plays a fundamental role in determining the structure of all astronomical bodies from the largest star to the tiniest atom. Although gravitation is one of the most familiar physical interactions of matter, it is at the same time one of the most mysterious and enigmatic. Everyone can witness the effects of gravity but no one really knows what gravitation is or how it works. Great mathematicians and physicists such as Sir Isaac Newton and Albert Einstein learned to measure the effects of gravity, but even these great thinkers could not really explain what gravity is.

In groups of people, there is a force nearly as pervasive as the physical force of gravity. It is the force of the group. The attitudes, opinions, and behavior of those around us can influence and affect our thinking as much as our core values. Group attitude is often called morale. The morale of a group is in a constant state of flux, moving and changing depending on how the group is reacting to various stimuli.

Although little is known about the source of gravity, the strength of its force is determined by its mass. Likewise, the percentage or number of people in a group, thinking a certain way determines the strength of groupthink. Almost everyone has heard his or her mother say at some time, "If everyone jumped off the cliff, would you?" The correct answer is probably "yes" for most people. Public or group opinion is a strong force and an individual must have high levels of self-assurance and confidence to make choices against the attitudes and beliefs of the group.

Groupthink affects the way people dress, the way they feel about important political decisions, and the way they react to others. Leaders and others wanting to understand the dynamics and motivation of group attitudes must understand the power and effect of groupthink.

The correct answer to "If everyone else jumps off the cliff, would you?" Is probably...yes!

Groups of people are never static in their beliefs, attitudes, values, or morale. Groups are constantly changing and evolving their opinions. Individuals enter a group with negative or positive self-talk, which changes under the power and influence of the groupthink. Unfortunately, positive self-talk is often diminished by negative groupthink. The groupthink can be directly opposite of what the individual wants to accomplish.

A demonstration I use in workshops and seminars to show the tendency of groups to drift in purpose and direction is an activity called "Floating Poles." In "Floating Poles", a rod (usually a curtain rod) is placed between several participants facing each other. Each person sticks out two index fingers and I place the rods on the top of each person's finger. The instructions are simple; keep your fingers touching the rod and lower the rod to the floor.

Typically, the group has little success lowering the pole. As each individual tries to keep their fingers touching the pole, the group's momentum makes the rod go up instead of down. The facilitator constantly barks orders for everyone to keep their fingers on the pole. Every person has an effect. The participants moving their fingers even slightly upward to make contact with the pole, causes the poles to move up instead of down. Many times the participants say the pole feels like it is floating on its own. Often, groups of people are drifting like the poles. Their self-talk may be trying to go one-way, but the momentum and force of groupthink takes them another.

A lesson from the furniture store

My experiences selling furniture in the family furniture store when I was a younger man taught me a lot about human behavior. Perry & McGee Furniture Company was a fixture in my hometown for nearly 70 years. My grandfather founded the store, and my father managed the business when I graduated from college. As the third generation to work in the store handling advertising and sales, I learned many things, but the dynamic of groupthink was probably the most profitable.

Our store, like many others, ran sales…periods of time when items were sold at a discount. These sales events varied in effectiveness depending on many factors including the economy, time of the year, weather, selection, and discounts. The most effective sales events, however, did not seem to be subject to these factors. These were limited time sales events we called "High Impact Events."

These special events generated a lot of attention and excitement. It was typical for the store to do a whole month's worth of business in one day during these sales. The store would close a day before these special sales. This gave us time to prepare and get ready for customers, but we also found the closed doors created tremendous excitement and anticipation. Many times, we would even paper the windows with brown paper so people could not peek in.

On the sale day, people would line up at the front door waiting to come in. Most times, they would rush to merchandise they wanted and line up at the cash register. When this kind of excitement occurred at the beginning of a sales event, we knew it would be a great day. We called it a "feeding frenzy" because customers would be so anxious to line up and buy. Fear of loss and hope for gain are strong motivators. Even today, retailers know the value of this powerful groupthink. They call it "Black Friday."

On these special days, the savings and discounts were of secondary importance compared to the fear many people had of being left out. Many people who normally would have taken hours or days to make up their minds would do so almost immediately. The impact of seeing so many other people buying, and the fear of "missing out" on a bargain, becomes too strong a motivator for the customer to resist.

The shopping experience stresses many people. Shopping goes beyond the tangible act of buying an item, taking it home, and enjoying it. Purchasing furniture had many facets of motivation. Some just wanted a piece of furniture while some expressed their style and creativity in their purchases. Shopping creates a great deal of anxiety. Buying meant making a decision, expressing their taste, bearing their soul, and putting their ability to bargain to the test. In short, people feared looking stupid. Effective selling required making the customer feel safe and having them feel they were making intelligent decisions. These "high impact" sale days were successful, in part, because people rushing to buy, made other shoppers feel safe. Groupthink is a powerful influence on individuals.

Any high school lunchroom in America provides an example of groupthink and how it works. In the school cafeteria a culture and belief system exists, that is tightly regulated and reinforced by the group, which says that the cafeteria food is bad. Almost any high school student, if asked, will tell you that their cafeteria food is terrible.

The quality of the food at the school's cafeteria is not the issue. Most school cafeterias serve excellent food. The culture of the high school lunchroom, though, is strong. There are peer rewards when complaining about cafeteria food. The more clever and creative the criticism of the food, the more positive feedback the student gets from their peers in the form of laughs, agreement, and approving nods. For a student to stand up in this culture and say, "I think the food is good and a great value," becomes a greater social risk than most want to take. Gourmet meals served by the finest chef's in the world would not challenge the stigma of this powerful culture, because the quality of the food is not nearly as important as approval from the group.

The lunchroom is an innocent example of how a culture affects the thinking and communication in a group. Unfortunately, this same dynamic can have more destructive consequences. Since the mid-1960's, it has been well documented and promoted that tobacco use has serious health consequences. Laws have been passed restricting the product's advertising and its use among minors. However, smoking is still prevalent in many groups. Many times people start smoking because the culture or groupthink in their group promotes it. The facts about health consequences, the expense of the habit, or the odor associated with tobacco use are no match for the power of this cultural influence.

Fashion is another aspect of our culture greatly influenced by groupthink. Look at any high school yearbook from any year and you will find kids dressing in ways, which will someday look ridiculous. We cannot help it… groupthink is too strong. As individual as teenagers strive to be, they have always dressed to look the same…even if they have to dress strangely.

Leadership's Role

Several years ago, I worked with an organization that had many different work groups. Some of these groups did similar work, but there was inconsistency in the performance of various departments. Two groups in particular were puzzling. They both had similar numbers. The employees had the same educational backgrounds and experience. Both groups engaged is similar kinds of work, yet one performed at high levels of productivity and the other was not.

The only difference in the two groups related to their direct supervision. Both supervisors were competent in their field, yet one was getting far superior results. The supervisor of the lower performing groups was very diligent in "keeping up" with his employees. He wanted to know every detail of their work and monitor it carefully. The other supervisor appeared to be doing much less, but his group consistently outperformed the other.

When interviewing individuals working in the two groups the difference in leadership became even more obvious. The lower performing group constantly waited for direction and approval, while the higher performing group got their work done. The higher performing group was convinced they were capable—in fact, they believed they were the most capable people in the organization. Much of their empowerment and performance came from their supervisor, who was always telling them, "You are the smartest people in this organization."

The high performing supervisor did many things well to prepare and empower the group, but the positive groupthink the supervisor created was contagious. The underperforming supervisor did little wrong, but the continual second-guessing of his employees developed a groupthink that encouraged doing the bare minimum. Worse, the employee in the underperforming group believed they were not capable of doing more than following his directives.

Developing open communications **(See Chapter 15, Dynamic of Communication)** involves leadership and a change in the groupthink. Every group has its own culture or belief system where opinions are valued and reinforced. These are not necessarily deep or spiritual ideals but instead may be extremely trivial and meaningless. Nonetheless, these outlooks are embraced and used by the group. The customs, habits, traditions, and artifacts characterizing a people or a social group define its culture. The culture includes the group's attitudes and beliefs about important aspects of its life. Culture is how things are done and are accepted among groups of people.

People in a group are influencing the opinions and attitudes of other people in a group. Leaders will need to identify, and take influence away from individuals with destructive attitudes while building on the strengths of the more positive influences in the group. Leaders must always structure their initiatives and communication in ways that are easily understood and interpreted by the individuals in the group.

Changing the culture of a group is a time intensive activity. A leader will need to substitute old behaviors, thinking, and practices with new, more productive habits. Success usually involves incremental alterations to the groupthink to allow the group to absorb the new thinking pattern.

Leadership's role in shaping groupthink is essential for organizational effectiveness. Leadership must be able to recognize the values of the group to help develop improved values. More than anything else, a leader must be able to identify and establish purpose for the group. The group must have a clear image of the purpose and the goals of the group. By continuously focusing attention and reminding people of the purpose the group has, the leader can help direct the groupthink in a positive direction.

Key Points

- Groupthink is a powerful force affecting the attitude of individuals in a group.
- To affect the attitude of individuals in the group it is necessary to affect the groupthink.
- Leadership's role is to establish and focus attention on the purpose of the group through Goals.

PART II

Transforming Ideas into Results

Planning is how leaders establish purpose, create vision, and motivate groups to success. Planning is also an effective technique to resolve conflicts, build consensus, and create a dynamic organization. Taking abstract ideas and transforming them into concrete and doable activities is one of the most powerful ways for a leader to build influence.

Chapter 6
Dynamic of Purpose:
Focusing on Why and How

"If you have a 'why' in your life, you can deal with almost any 'how'"
Friedrich Nietzsche

When my 15-year-old daughter learned to play golf, I was reminded of the importance of **Why** and **How**. Daughters do not usually take advice from their dad about clothes, keeping a clean room, driving, social life, and many other activities for which their dads have an interest. Surprisingly, this lack of appreciation for my wisdom extended to the golf course as well.

While playing the 12th hole at our local golf course, she hit several shots in a row heavy, which means she hit the ground before the ball. When I asked if she wanted any help, she snapped back that she did not. She continued by curtly saying, "I know what I'm doing...I'm hitting behind the ball." She was right, but she was making a fundamental mistake common almost all beginning golfers. I often made the same mistake at her age.

As a 15-years-old golfer, Leroy Fitzwater the local golf pro took an interest in my golf game. He often ask how I was playing and occasionally came to the practice area to watch me hit a few balls. One day, while battling a particularly wicked hook, which means the ball was going left of the target, Leroy came up and asked, "How are you doing?"

"I'm hooking it," was my sharp reply.

Leroy said, "You're answering the wrong question. You're telling me what's happening. If you want to be a good player, you have to be able to answer **why** **it's** **happening**."

What is happening is not as important as **why** something is happening.

That lesson in golf always stuck with me. What you are doing or what is happening is not as important as *why something is*

happening. Golf, in a large part, is about figuring out the reasons and root causes for bad golf shots then making appropriate corrections. The fact my daughter hit behind the ball was not the issue as much as the reasons *why* she was doing this. Was she standing too close? Was she moving her head? Was she dipping her shoulder? The *why* or the reasons behind the results were the real issue...what was really important. Once the *why* of the golf swing is figured out, the player can concentrate on the *how.*

Life is like golf in that way. We're so busy explaining *what* is happening, we fail to address the more important questions of *why* something is happening and *how* do we affect a more positive outcome. Learning to understand *why*, something is happening, is essential in developing a vision of the current reality.

Communication describes and defines human existence. It has three main functions: to inform, to inquire, and to persuade. Embedded in these three functions are the **essential information** of **who, what, when, where, why**, and **how**. These elements are useful in all types of communication and almost anything a person needs to know can be describe by these six important questions.

Who, What, When, and Where help us answer the more important questions of Why and How.

I once taught a workshop on advertising to small businesses. In advertising, *who, what, when, where, why*, and *how* are of paramount importance. While searching for materials and examples of advertising, to use in class, I ran across an extraordinary piece of advertising. This mail-out brochure was beautifully done, well laid out, and nicely printed. The ad effectively generated interest, had good product information, and excellent examples of prices with deep discounts. It explained *what* the sales event was and *when* the event would happen. The ad even did a good job of explaining *why* customers should buy and *how* they could make purchases. Only two things were missing...the name of the store and where it was located. The omission of these pieces of essential information (the *who* and the *where*) made this advertising effort completely ineffective and probably a total waste of advertising budget.

Successful communication requires addressing these vital questions. There is, however, a hierarchy or level of importance to this essential information. *who*, *what*, *when*, and *where* questions are factual, objective pieces of information. This **observable information** is easily verified and concrete. A person can see *who* it is, observe *what* it is, look at a clock or calendar to see *when* it is and notice, by observation or a map, *where* it is. There is usually little argument or disagreement about these factual, objective, and observable components of essential information. When my daughter told me she was hitting the golf shot heavy, there was no disagreement. The results were observable and obvious. *What* was happening was apparent. To be successful, she would also need to reason *why*.

Dynamics of Information

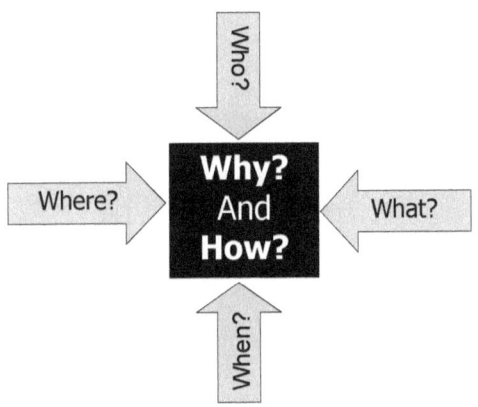

The question *why*, however, requires intuitive analysis instead of observable data. It is still essential information in creating vision and seeing reality, but *why* requires reason instead of observation. *Why* is philosophic and intangible. Direct observation becomes nearly impossible. Opinions may differ widely about *why*. My daughter and I could easily agree on what was happening to her golf shots. She was hitting them heavy. However, we could easily disagree on *why* she was hitting them that way. The question of *why* is a higher order or more meaningful piece of essential information. To effectively analyze information, you must be able to observe, document, and collect data about the *who*, *what*, *when*, and *where* then synthesize those facts into the cause or *why* something is happening. The inability to analyze the observable information into the root causes can make a leader data rich and analysis poor. Thinking dynamically involves using the observable information with reasoning and logic to determine why.

Why is a question of purpose and the important question to ask to find the root causes of problems and challenges to develop solutions. Purpose motivates, directs, and even inspires individuals and groups. For leaders, the purpose or the *why* should be clear. Leaders focus attention on the purpose of the group to create positive inertia in moving the group toward positive goals.

Evolution of Information

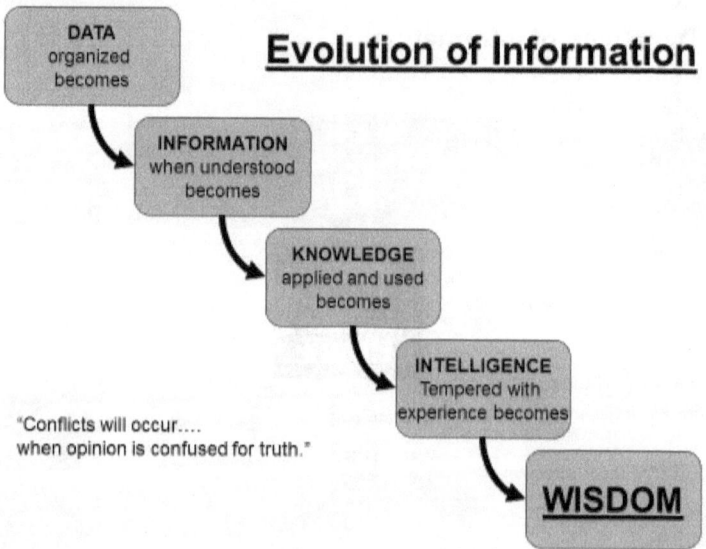

Collecting data and facts are essential tools to answering the important questions of *who, what, when,* and *where* to better determine the *why* and *how.* Data, however, is of little use unless transformed into analysis leading to useful information. Data, or the raw tidbits of information that can be collected, needs to be organized to become knowledge. In accounting systems, this synthesis of numbers happens routinely. Accounting systems rely on properly handling source documents—those pieces of paper documenting a transaction has occurred. Those pieces of data are entered into a general journal where the financial information is sorted chronologically and then categorically. Once the raw data has been organized chronologically and categorically into ledgers and accounts, the financial information can be summarized into an Income Statement and a Balance Sheet, which then can be used in making decisions. Data organized becomes information. When information is understood, it becomes knowledge. When knowledge is applied and used it becomes intelligence. Intelligence tempered with experience then becomes wisdom.

Eroding of Purpose

Purpose provides direction for individuals, groups, or organizations. Answering, analyzing, and determining *why* becomes a constant and vital quest for leaders because people and organizations can experience an **eroding of purpose**. Good intentions, goals, objectives, and values sometimes evaporate with the passing of time.

Sociologists and anthropologists have pointed to a pattern of change, which tends to occur in institutions from one generation to the next. First generations are made up of the "founding fathers and mothers" who establish organizations with a clear and common purpose. They are drawn together by a vision of something new, for which they have committed and sometimes sacrificed to start. The second generation is made up of individuals who remember the original purpose of the group and are close to that purpose because of their direct contact with the originators. By the third, fourth, or fifth generation there evolves a trend in which people fail to remember the original motivations and purpose. [6] What were innovative activities in the past become routine and repetitive without much questioning or reasoning why.

Eroding of purpose happens in all types of organizations including educational settings. One day I was visiting with a colleague about a new master's degree program he was pursuing in which he was genuinely excited. Both of us had been involved in several degree programs and had complained in the past about the relevance and value of some programs. He mentioned the class he was taking now had a clear purpose, and the classes in the program seemed to relate well to each other.

---

[6] Hiebert, Paul, G. *Missions and the Renewal of the Church*, William B Eerdmans Pub. Co. Grand Rapids, Michigan, 1983

We often talked about other programs we had taken where courses seemed disjointed, or even worse, repetitive. We talked about the difference in this program and why it seemed more relevant. Was it the teacher, the facility, the attitude of the learner, or the attitude of the other students in the class? None of these factors appeared to be dramatically different from other experiences. He did note one important difference…this was a brand new degree program. Many of the professors currently teaching in the program were involved in its design. This program was better because its purpose was still fresh and clear. There had been no eroding of purpose…yet.

Over time, the educators who originally design programs can leave the institution or assume different duties. There is always a possibility for educational programs to erode from their original intent or purpose. Teachers sometimes forgot or maybe didn't know how their class affected the whole program. Teachers sometimes teach what they thought was important instead of the intent and purpose of the whole program. Thinking in isolation, the purpose of the whole can be lost. Educators know programs must be reviewed periodically and adjusted to ensure they are purposeful and relevant to the learner. The essential information *why* is about purpose and direction. Determining *why* is an ongoing endeavor.

Schools are not the only victims of eroding purpose. Businesses often forget purpose. A dynamic new business venture almost always begins with a strong focus on customers and meeting their needs. Over time, companies can lose this focus. Many times business organizations are operated for the convenience of the people working in the business instead of the real boss, the customer.

Cornelius Vanderbilt was a noted railroad tycoon of the 19th century. Upon his death, he was the richest man in the United States. Vanderbilt, however, never considered himself to be in the railroad business…he was in the transportation business.

Vanderbilt began his career from humble beginnings with a $100 loan. His first enterprise was delivering freight on the rivers of the northeast using sailboats. Later, after seeing the success of Robert Fulton's steam ship, he sold his sailboats and went into the steamboat business. Actually, he was still in the same business, the transportation business, using a new and improved method to meet the needs. Later he entered the railroad business but still the prime business, the purpose, was transportation.

The railroad industry as an institution in America has greatly diminished in contemporary times partly because railroad companies believed they were in the railroad business and forgot they were in the transportation business. Resources were allocated based on the way things had been. Decisions were made with considerations for the convenience of the railroad industry instead of the customer. Truck and air transportation made inroads while in many ways the railroad industry forgot its purpose...transportation. [7]

WHY IS THE QUESTION OF PURPOSE

Why is often the hardest question. It requires vigilant self-analysis and a clear vision of where the group or person is and where they want to go. *Why* means continually defining and redefining purpose. Leadership is almost synonymous with purpose. Leaders must help determine what is important to the group and help focus attention on those core beliefs. Effective leaders create clear vision of purpose for the group.

True genius is to transform the complicated into the simple. Organizations and the people in them have bureaucratic tendencies that can create stifling controlling force. People sometimes take simple purposes and build them into more intricate and complex operations.

True genius is to transform the complicated into the simple...not the other way around.

The United States of America was established with a one page document called the Declaration of Independence. This declaration concisely stated the purpose, ideals, and beliefs of the European settlers in the New World. Several years later, the United States Constitution was adopted to govern the new nation consisting of several pages. Since that beginning, the number of laws and regulations has multiplied to the point no one, including

---

[7] Lane, Wheaton J., *Commodore Vanderbilt*, Alfred A. Knopf Co., New York, New York, 1942

lawmakers, know the whole scope of the law. Periodically a leader arrives on the scene to refocus attention on the purpose and beliefs the society values.

Memorable speeches by great leaders of American history have made complicated issues clear and simple. Abraham Lincoln was wrong when he stated in his Gettysburg Address, "The world will little note nor long remember what we say here…" The world did remember that short and simple speech describing the horror of war and the hope for the future with the phrase, "that this nation, under God, shall have a new birth of freedom."

Thomas Jefferson, when drafting the Declaration of Independence, summed up the future of a continent when he penned this simple idea, "We hold these truths to be self-evident, that all men are created equal, that they are endowed by their Creator with certain unalienable Rights, that among these are Life, Liberty and the pursuit of Happiness."

Franklin D. Roosevelt guided a nation through the despair of a great depression by many actions and words. His simple statement, "We have nothing to fear, but fear itself" created hope for a return to the American dream.

Martin Luther King Jr. gave what many consider one of the greatest of American speeches and summed up the realities of his day with the hope for tomorrow with the simple phrase, "I have a dream."

Leadership is not about having all the answers, but it is about asking the right questions for determining *why* a group exists. For leaders, finding purpose is finding direction and building influence. Help determine the purpose for a group, and you influence them toward a destination. Understanding an individual's purpose puts them closer to knowing the dynamic causing them to act and react the way they do.

If *why* is a philosophic piece of essential information, then *how* is the technical component. *How* deals with planning, strategies, tactics, and actions. It uses the other elements of essential information and is dependent on them. **<u>Who</u>, <u>what</u>, <u>when</u>, and <u>where</u> help determine <u>why</u> in order to decide <u>how</u>.**

There are always more people that can tell you *why* something cannot be done than those who can tell you *how* it can be done. The economic principles of scarcity, supply and demand (another dynamic by the way) explain why individuals who can tell you *how* are more valuable.

The higher-order elements of essential information, *why* and *how*, are about purpose and possibilities. When people challenge themselves with thinking about *why* and *how*, they motivate themselves with purpose and possibilities. Skipping the observable information and jumping right to *how* can be a mistake. For the *how* to be effective the *why* must be known. The observable information, *who*, *what*, *when*, and *where*, provide vision and perspective to help determine *why*.

Why and *how* should always be the focus of leadership. Leaders who think dynamically should always concentrate on *why* and *how*. One of the primary roles of a leader is to help the group establish purpose to focus and refocus the group's attention on that purpose. Answering the question of *why* fundamentally helps in finding that purpose.

Key Points

- *Who*, *What*, *When*, and *Where* are observable information and a tool for creating a vision of the current reality.
- *Why* is a philosophic question of purpose.
- *How* is the technical question of getting things accomplished.
- To effectively manage information a leader should first gather data and facts, then analyze the root causes of issues, and finally develop action plans based on this hierarchy of information.

Chapter 7
Dynamic of Aligned Action:
Turning Diversity into Results

"Where all think alike, no one thinks very much."

Walter Lippman

Leaders need followers. It is a prerequisite of leadership. Various groups and sub-groups comprise an organization, but fundamentally, leaders lead people. Many factors including strategic purpose, morale, and direction affected a group. Possibly the most important skill for a leader is the ability to build consensus and move a group toward a common purpose.

The Egyptian pharaoh Khufu of the 4th dynasty built the Great Pyramid in Giza around 2560 BC. When constructed, the Great Pyramid was 481 feet high. It ranked as the tallest structure on Earth for more than 4,468 years. The Eiffel Tower built in 1889 became the first fabricated structure of any kind to surpass the Great Pyramid in height. The first stone building, however, to surpass the ancient Egyptians was the Singer Building at Broadway and Bourne Street in Lower Manhattan, when constructed in May of 1908 at a height of 612 feet. The Singer Building was the tallest structure for only a year until the Metropolitan Life Tower surpassed it in 1909. The Singer Building lasted only 60 years and was demolished in 1968.

Diversity of opinions and ideas is the foundation to successful planning.

The Great Pyramid, built with a broad base, has lasted for over 44 centuries. The Singer building replacing it as the "world's tallest" was built with a narrow base and modern construction techniques. It lasted only 6 decades.

Diversity is like the base of a pyramid—broad, inclusive, and strong. With its broad base, a pyramid takes time and effort to construct. It would be quicker to build a structure by stacking stones one on another, but the geometry of stacking stones limits the height the building can obtain. In working with groups of people, it is harder to plan and construct a shared vision for the group but this is the foundation to success. What seems to be the easy way to lead (just telling people what to do) severely inhibits a group's ability to achieve their potential.

Leaders cannot just "tell people what to do," they must work with members of the group to build agreement on values, desires, and ideals to move in a direction most beneficial to the whole. The art of leadership involves integrating the ideas and outlooks of the many individuals into a harmonious accord of shared purpose.

Leaders need vision and the ability to analyze the current realities facing the group. They also need to be able to identify and manage the available resources of the group. In creating vision, perspective is a valuable tool. **(See Chapter 2, Dynamic of Vision)** Understanding the value of the many opinions, ideas, beliefs, and points-of-view is a method leaders can use to get a perspective of the current reality.

How Groups Work By Aligned Actions

Moving groups by aligned actions involves both driving force and controlling force. Ideas generated by the diversity, ingenuity, and creativity of the individual members becomes a strong driving force. The challenge for leaders is to transform the driving force of diversity into positive actions and results by using the controlling force of focused planning. Leaders can control and balance the driving force of diversity by creating vision, establishing purpose, defining mission, and establishing goals.

Groups succeed, fail, or stagnate depending on a leader's ability to establish purpose and achieve constructive actions among members of the group. Typical group activity begins in what seems to be a chaotic way with a myriad of ideas, opinions, beliefs, values, and desires shared by the many individuals in a group. Some of these viewpoints may be strong, while others will be more apathetic. Some members of the group will agree and have very similar thoughts, while others may have strongly conflicting ideas.

This process of generating ideas is like raw energy: a genesis of force that starts a group moving. All groups go through this process of individuals proposing and advocating ideas while trying to influence other members of the group. Without leadership, this process fails to evolve past brainstorming.

Sometimes the group may vacillate between differing opinions as it tests ideas. Other times some individuals will champion ideas and take off in a direction without buy-in or support from others. The group may have to reset itself as it tries to reestablish purpose. Many times the members of the group get so frustrated that the process dissolves as group planning fails.

To succeed, the energy from the ideas and brainpower generated by the individuals in the group must be transformed toward a common direction. Compromise, negotiation, and open communication **(See Chapter 15, Dynamic of Communication)** must be employed to elicit all of the ideas, values, and desires from the group. Everyone still has their own thoughts and personalities, but the group's energies and activities must be focused toward common goals and purpose.

Dynamic of Aligned Action

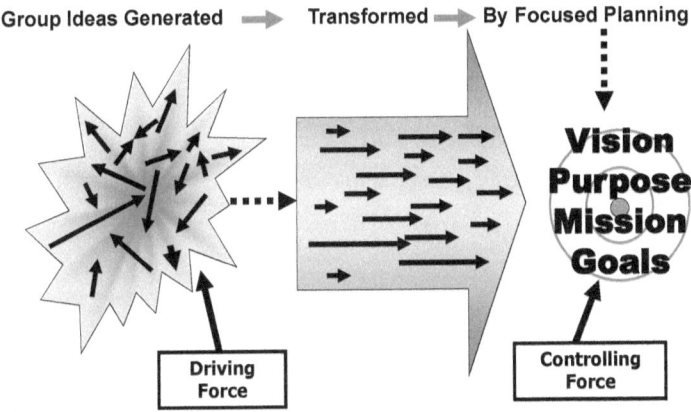

The energy from the ideas generated by the group becomes transformed in momentum for accomplishment by focused planning. The driving force of ideas is focused by the controlling force of planning and purpose. The future vision of where the group ideally wants to go, its purpose, the mission of the group, and shared goals come from a leader's ability to transform the raw energy of the group's ideas through planning. If a leader can achieve nothing else, they should strive to build consensus and a shared vision of the preferable future for the group.

Key Points

- Learn to appreciate and respect the power of diversity in a group.
- Work to get all ideas and opinions on the table from all the affected members of the group.
- Look for ways to tie the ideas of the many into a shared vision by focusing on the group's purpose and on group goals.

Chapter 8
Dynamic of Planning:
Turning Ideas Into Results

> *"In preparing for battle I have always found plans are useless,*
> *but planning is indispensable."*
>
> Dwight D. Eisenhower

Planning answers three fundamental questions:

1. **Where are we now?**
2. **Where do we want to be?**
3. **How do we get there?**

Planning is fundamental to almost everything a person does. It is perhaps the biggest factor in determining long-term success or failure. Whether formal or informal, conscience or subconscious, the dynamic of planning is occurring constantly. Planning is the process determining what needs to be done and how. Many fail to understand planning or plan effectively, but the dynamic is at work just the same. For leaders, planning becomes an effective driving force to influence a group to a more preferable future, a controlling force to monitor a group's progress toward obtaining objectives, an effective tool to resolve conflicts, a means to establish purpose for a group, a way to get people on the same page, and a method to implement positive change.

The planning process involves the dynamic effects of driving force and controlling force. The imagination, desires, values, and ideals provide driving force in the process, while the current situation and available resources become the constraining or controlling forces. Too much driving force (big dreams) without sufficient resources will result in frustrations and chaos. However, stagnation and low achievement occur if the driving force is much less than the controlling force. Effective planners and leaders continually balance the wants of the group with the resources available. This can be achieved by increasing or decreasing the driving forces or adding to the capacity of the controlling forces.

A plan is not a qualitative—it can be good or bad. The dynamic of planning is at work in a successful business, but the same dynamic is involved in the plan leading to disaster, as well. Planning happens all the time. Unfortunately, few people understand the dynamic of planning and how to use planning to succeed. Many people plan to fail without ever realizing it!

Dynamic of Planning

1. Where are we now?
2. Where do we want to be?
3. How do we get there?

The process of planning takes an individual or group from **abstract** ideals, values, desires, and future dreams to specific, **concrete** tasks, which must be done to achieve goals. It transforms what a person or group believes, dreams, and envisions for the future and combines it with the current situation and available resources to establish goals, develop strategies, and implement tactics. The results are then evaluated to see how they affect the new current situation and available resources for future planning. Planning is an on-going and evolving process. The process takes the broad ideas or vision essential for planning and condenses or focuses the vision into doable activities.

Individuals or groups may have many planning dynamics occurring simultaneously. A group may have a strategic or long-range plan with numerous tactical or short-term planning processes occurring to support the bigger plan. A group can also have several strategic initiatives working simultaneously. Plans are continually evolving to meet the ever-changing current situation and available resources.

Imagination

The planning process starts in an abstract, creative, and broad way by thinking (and even dreaming) about the possibilities and the most preferable future. **Imagination** in the planning process is about visualizing things the way we would like them to be. This phase is almost like pre-planning because it is not concerned with the constraints of "where we are" or "how we get there." Reality is suspended as people are challenged to envision all they can be and all they want to be. Imagining requires contemplation and reflection about the things truly important to the individual or the group.

This abstract phase of planning considers the values, beliefs, desires, ideals, and future of the individual or group. When imagining, people must decide what they value and what is really most important. Values, beliefs, ideals, and desires are personal preferences with varying degrees of intensity.

After imagining the preferred future and analyzing these personal values in composing that future, the purpose of the planning begins to emerge. Purpose represents what is important. It is the "WHY" motivating individuals and groups. **(See Chapter 6, Dynamic of Purpose)** The stronger the purpose, the more focused an individual or group becomes in pursuing the goals in the planning process. As the German philosopher Friedrich Nietzsche said, "If you have a why in your life, you can deal with any how."

Anything created was first imagined.

Imagining involves envisioning the ideal future. It is the driving force in the planning dynamic. Everything that has been accomplished was first imagined. Taking the time to dream about an ideal future can be a strong motivator and driving force for an individual or group.

Planning Example: Imagination

Creating an image of the preferred future is different for each person depending on his or her values, desires and ideal future. For examples of planning, the game of golf will be used to illustrate how the planning dynamic works.

I've played golf since I was twelve years old. I love the game. The smell of the fresh cut grass, the shadows on the course at dusk, the sound of a well-hit shot, and the exhilaration of making a long putt are all attractions. My dream is to be a championship golfer, to win, to play with Tiger Woods and Jack Nicklaus. I fantasize about being in the fairway on the last hole of an important championship and hitting a two iron ten feet from the pin to win it all.

When creating a vision, it is okay to dream and even fantasize. The purpose is to identify what is important to the individual. Realize the level of importance and interest will differ depending on the person. My wife does not fantasize about me playing golf...she probably fantasizes about me cutting the grass without being asked.

Finding Purpose for a Group

One of the most important aspects of leadership is defining purpose for a group. One of the by-products of the imagination phase of planning should be a clearer definition of the purpose of the plan and a better idea about the purpose of the group.

Establishing purpose involves

- The ideals the group is **passionate** about
- The **measurements** of success for the group
- The **unique strengths** of the group.

During the planning process a leader should be able to discover what the group is passionate about, know what their measures of success are, and determine what they can do that is unique, different, and better than anyone else. These three factors are useful tools in establishing purpose for a group.

Current Situation and Available Resources

If the imagination phase of planning is the driving force, the current situation and available resource to pursue the dream are the constraining or controlling force. The imagining phase of planning is not concerned with reality, but instead challenges the individual to dream and visualize a preferable future. The abstract thinking involved in imagining, however, must be tempered with the concrete realities of the current situation and available resources.

Having a vision of the future requires a clear vision of the present. Developing the objectivity to analyze the current situation is a significant challenge. **(See Chapter 2, Dynamic of Vision)** Imagining is the fun part of planning because the realities of the current situation and the available resources have been ignored. Answering the first planning question (Where are we now?) is a critical step in effective planning.

Imagining the future by analyzing the values, desires, and ideals of the group is the driving force in planning. The current reality and the available resources become the controlling force. Knowing where you are is the first practical step in effective planning. If you do not know where you are, it is impossible to chart a course to take you where you want to be.

The challenge in determining the current situation is difficult because it requires objectivity. Every person or organization has different talents and abilities as well as some weaknesses. Objectively establishing the current reality helps determine the best and most realistic goals to pursue. Past performance, strengths, weaknesses, resources, attitude, intelligence, and personal reputation have a great influence on a group's capacity to achieve. The current situation may include factors such as financial condition, attitude or morale, ability to adapt to meet challenges, competitive environment, and physical resources to be used in achieving goals. Available resources include factors such as: financial resources, political resources, time, experience, expertise, geographic location, available personnel, and capacity for growth.

Objectivity is essential when determining the current situation and available resources. Feelings and emotions provide the passion needed in imagining the preferable future, but they are a barrier to objectively seeing the reality of the current situation and available resources. To determine the reality of the current situation and available resources, it is helpful to deal with data and facts.

Financial statements, culture surveys, customer service feedback, and other documentation of performance are helpful. Finding other people who will give viewpoints about the strengths and weaknesses, combined with willingness to accept the truth about what others think, can also be a great asset in developing the objectivity needed to establish the current situation.

Effective planning requires objective analysis of the reality of the current situation and the available resources with which a person has to work. Objectively looking at the past, developing a list of strengths and weaknesses, and getting a perspective from other people using open communication are all strategies, which should be employed. Developing a "view from the press box" **(See Chapter 2, Dynamic of Vision)** and consciously learning to see things the way they really are instead of how we want them to be are also good planning habits. The imagining phase of planning is fun and exciting. Establishing the current situation and available resources can be sobering and even depressing. To get where you want to go, however, you have to know where you are.

Planning Example:
Establishing Current Situation & Available Resources

When speaking to groups, I like to surprise them by stating I was in the United States Open golf championship, held in Tulsa, Oklahoma in 1977. It's true, but people assume since I play golf that I played in the U.S. Open championship. Actually, I got to carry score banners for the players. I was "in" the U.S. Open but not as a player. This experience as a young, ambitious player who wanted to be better showed me the gap between how good I thought I was and how great the best players in the world were. It also showed my current situation and available resources were not sufficient at the time to accomplish the vision I had created without significant improvement.

Goal Setting

The values, desires, and ideals imagined by an individual or group are the driving force in the planning dynamic. The current reality and available resources are the controlling force. **Goals are the reconciliation of all that an individual or group wants to be** (Imagining) **and what they have to work with** (Current Situation and Available Resources). Goal setting is a compromise between dreams and reality.

Goals are like a compass, which guide an oceangoing ship. The ship may have to veer off-course to avoid storms, icebergs, or other ships, but the compass always points in the same direction so the ship can get back on course and to its destination. Goals and planning help people get back on course and stay on course...even when they have to make detours in life.

The impact of goal setting in individual success is well known. Goal setting requires imagination, visionary thinking, and maybe a little dreaming but tempered with the reality of the current situation and available resources. Goals should be

> **Goals are the reconciliation between all that we want...and what we have to work with.**

challenging yet obtainable. Goals are broad statements of direction in the planning process, but they need to be specific and include a timetable. A goal without a deadline is a dream; setting goals without setting a time guideline reduces the chance the goal will be reached. Goals also need to be measurable to determine progress. Goals, which are obtainable, challenging, specific, timed, and measurable, should also be written. Written goals increase the effectiveness of goal setting. Goals are generally long-range objectives requiring more than a day or two to reach. Written goals serve as a reminder of what the individual or group has chosen to pursue. Written goals also help a group avoid conflicts and misunderstandings by making the future objectives concrete and clear.

Planning Example:
Goal Setting

My vision of being a championship golfer and competing with Tiger and the Golden Bear may have been a little bold based on the natural ability given to me (and my level of determination.) When I created my vision, I realized I had other things I valued more than golf. Having a family and staying close to home were higher priorities for me than globetrotting around the world playing golf.

Now it's time for me to set my golfing goals based on the vision, but tempered with my current situation and available resources. I want to set goals that are obtainable, challenging, specific, timed, measurable, and written.

A poorly written goal might sound like this. I want to be a good golfer. *(Too vague, may not be obtainable, not measurable, no time limit, and may not be challenging enough.)*

A better-written goal might sound like this. I will improve my average score 10 strokes (obtainable, specific and measurable) by Labor Day of this year (timed) and compete for the club championship (challenging).

Strategies

The most important question answered by the planning process is "How do we get there?" Group planning often fails when it comes to deciding how things get done. Many people will give opinions about the direction of the group or point out the strengths and weaknesses. Goal setting gets more difficult because it involves restrictions based on the current situation and available resources. Goal setting also involves making a commitment to a direction and many people do not like that level of accountability.

Strategies involve the **long-term use and allocation of resources** to accomplish goals and objectives. Imagining requires creativity and the courage to dream. Establishing the current situation and analyzing the available resources involves being objective and seeing things the way they really are. Goal setting tempers the ideal future with the reality of the current situation. Challenging and worthwhile goals many times reveal gaps between the desired objectives, the current situation, and available resources. Strategies are the method to close those gaps and increase the available resources needed to accomplish goals.

The decision to invest in education and self-improvement is an example of a strategy. Many people in our present society decide to make career changes sometime in their working life. Often the kind of job a person has set as their goal will require additional training or education. A strategy of

Strategies deal with the **long-term use and allocation of resources** to accomplish goals and objectives.

devoting time and financial resources to go back to school to close this ability gap will be needed. The allocation of resources can be in the form of time, money, material, or focus. A wise student will look at the return on investment they will get for the strategic use of their resources.

Strategic planning (an often-overused term) deals with the long-term accomplishment of goals. In World War II, the B-17 Flying Fortress and the B-29 Super Fortress were ***strategic*** bombers. Their mission was to destroy munitions factories, ball-bearing plants, hydroelectric facilities, and other assets, which would help the enemy wage war. Sometimes a mission had little effect on the daily battle the soldier on the battlefield was fighting. The planes would fly overhead and not drop a single bomb close to the fighting. The mission was strategic to accomplish long-term goals. Strategies are not about fighting the battle but winning the war.

Strategies dedicate the long-term use of resources. Effective strategic planners analyze factors influencing success or failure, use identified strengths, improve weaknesses, and identify barriers to reach the established goals. Strategies are a commitment to long-term objectives, and each goal may require using multiple strategies.

Planning Example: Strategies

After creating my vision of golfing excellence and tempering it with the current situation and available resources to set goals, I now have to start doing something to get where I want to go with my golf game.

GOAL

I will improve my average score 10 strokes (obtainable, specific and measurable*)* by Labor Day of this year (timed*)* and compete for the club championship (challenging).

Strategy 1: I will pay $500 to go to a golf camp and take lessons from a professional (allocating resources) because I don't really know how to play (assessing current situation).

Strategy 2: I will practice 10 hours a week and play 3 rounds a week (allocating resources).

Tactics

The focus of the planning dynamic begins to change when determining goals, allocating resources, and developing strategies. What began as abstract thinking and an objective look at the current reality now narrows toward the tactics and specific actions, which needed to reach the objective. Accomplishments are comprised of a multitude of actions. Actions are the manifestation of what a person really believes. It is important to demonstrate actions aligned and consistent with stated goals. Goals should reflect things the person or group value and desire.

Think about making a trip to a supermarket. The motivation may be as simple as being hungry. It could be a more sophisticated driving force like a desire for gourmet cooking or a party for the weekend. The current situation would include things like the distance to the store, the condition of the roads, or the weather. The available resources might include the mode of transportation available or determining if the family car has enough gas. The supermarket would be the goal and the chosen route to the store would be the strategy. In this illustration, the specific turns, braking, and acceleration would be the tactics. People can know exactly where they want to go, and have a good strategy to get there, but they still must follow through with the actions.

Earlier, we mentioned the role of strategic bombers in World War II. Another World War II airplane was the P-51 Mustang. Many times the mission of the P-51 was to give tactical support to the strategic bomber. This little plane did not bomb factories but it did allow the bigger aircraft to accomplish its goal. The P-51's would also provide direct or **tactical** support for those troops fighting on the ground. The soldier in battle might not see the immediate benefit of the strategic bomber, but the tactical air support was helping right then and was having an immediate impact on the battle. Tactics are the **little things that must be done to accomplish the bigger goals** in life.

> # Tactics are the little things that must be done to accomplish the bigger goals in life.

In group planning, the individual actions of the members are like the glue that binds a team together. When the actions of the various individuals are coordinated toward goals and organizational purpose, tremendous synergy and concerted efforts can be achieved.

The dynamic of the planning process goes from broad ideals, which transform into specific actions to get results. Another thing happening in the planning dynamic is **time compression**. In the imagining phase of planning, time is vague. Imagining comprises abstract ideals of what the future may be like. In the goal-setting phase, time becomes an issue but usually the time-frame for accomplishing a goal is

> # Time is a strategic resource that must be allocated, but tactically, planning becomes preparation in using time effectively.

fairly long. Strategies involve allocation of resources, including time. When the planning process gets to the tactical phase, planned activities happen fast, and time becomes a significant factor. Time is a valuable resource, often is understated or ignored in the planning process. We generally understand the importance of deadlines, but we forget the opportunity cost of time. If we devote time to one objective, something else generally is forfeited.

The time compression is like a basketball team preparing for a tournament. Goals are established based on ability and competition. Practices occur using available time and resources to bridge the gaps between the current situation and the goals. The coach may use the practice time to work on defense, rebounding, shooting, or some other aspect of the game. When it is game time, however, the preparation must be manifest on the floor by doing the things practiced. A specific play can no longer be repeated over and over until it is perfected. The action in the game is happening right then, in real-time. The team may have practiced for hours preparing for the last five seconds of the game, but when the game is on, there are no longer hours to practice, just the five seconds to perform. The specific actions and performance of the players become the tactical part of winning the game or achieving the season's goal.

Tactics and actions are how things get done. Too many people think they are planning just because they come up with some goals, which appeal to them. Real planning is a continual process that is manifest in work.

Planning is a continual process that is manifest in work.

Tactics are the daily actions supporting the strategies and goals, which have been set. Tactics demonstrate what is really important. To succeed and accomplish, a person must do the little things (Tactics) to accomplish the big things (Goals.) To excel at planning and in life, you must decide what is wanted (Imagining and Goals,) then decide what needs to be done (Strategies,) and then do it (Tactics.)

Planning Example: Tactics

| Now it's time for me to act. I have to put my effort behind the vision created and the goals established.

GOAL

I will improve my average score 10 strokes (obtainable, specific and measurable) by Labor Day of this year (timed) and compete for the club championship (challenging).

Strategy 1: I will pay $500 to go to a golf camp and take lessons from a professional (allocating resources) because I don't really know how to play (assessing current situation).

   Tactic 1:1 Work one month of overtime to pay for golf camp.

   Tactic 1:2 Take one week of vacation to attend golf camp.

Strategy 2: I will practice 10 hours a week and play 3 rounds a week (allocating resources).

   Tactic 2:1 Will give up television at night and get up one hour earlier each morning to practice.

   Tactic 2:2 Will work on putting 2 hours each week.

   Tactic 2:3 Will work on tee shots 2 hours each week.

   Tactic 2:4 Will work on iron shots 2 hours each week.

   Tactic 2:5 Will work on short game 4 hours each week.

   Tactic 2:6 Will play competitive rounds on Mondays, Fridays, and Saturdays.

Determining the current situation and the available resources can be revealing. Imagining and setting goals can be fun. The real work of a successful planning process is determining what needs to be done to accomplish the goals and sometimes who will do it. Strategies require allocating resources and tactics require implementing action to obtain goals. Many individuals and groups fail at this point in the planning process. Objectively determining the current situation, writing down goals, then implementing strategies and tactics will turn into good habits for success. Strategies deal with the allocation of resources to accomplish long-term goals while tactics deal with the daily action needed to reach goals.

Actions, Results and Evaluation

Planning is a continuous, circular cycle. An individual or group may manage multiple plans at any one time. The planning process goes from abstract ideas to concrete actions—from broad ideals to specific actions. Results are evaluated because they then affect the new current situation and available resources. The dynamic is active and is constantly evolving.

For example, a person decides to make a career change and determines they need more education. If they are successful, they will find at the end of the process they are more educated and have a better current situation than before. Maybe the higher education level increases the pay and thus increases the available resources with which a person has to use.

> **The planning process takes abstract ideas and turns them into concrete actions.**

The result of planning and experiences gained will usually have an effect on the current situation and available resources in planning. Life is not a destination as much as a journey and the planning question, "Where are we now?" is elastic and always changing. Leaders who understand the planning dynamic know the importance of objectively analyzing their strengths, weaknesses, opportunities, and challenges. They also know the value of planning in creating inertia and a focus of purpose for the group.

Planning Example:
Actions, Results and Evaluation

The process is over...for now. My work and dedication to my golf game has resulted in lowering my score 8 strokes. On Labor Day, I finished in the top ten of the tournament. I learned that putting and my nerves (choking) were the biggest barriers to my success.

I am an 8-strokes-a-round better player than before. Breaking the habit of watching television every evening and getting into the habit of waking up early is giving me more time to practice and do other things.

New Vision

I want to enjoy playing golf and encourage my children to play golf with me.

Old Goal

I will improve my average score 10 strokes *(obtainable, specific and measurable)* by Labor Day of this year *(timed)* and compete for the club championship *(challenging)*.

New Goals

- I will improve by 2 more strokes this year.
- I will take my two kids to play golf with me this year.
- I'm going to skip the club championship this year and go on a family vacation. (I discovered I didn't really like the pressure of competitive golf.)

Planning is dynamic. Goals have evolved to fit my new vision, current situation, and available resources.

GROUP PLANNING CHALLENGES

Although the planning dynamic functions the same for individual and group planning, there are some inherit challenges to the group planning process. Group dynamics can vary depending on the personality, motivation, and level of conflict within an organization. It is easy to get sidetracked and thrown off balance when facilitating a group plan.

A few questions a leader wants to consider before the initial planning meetings include:

- **Does the group's plan need to address long-range vision or short-term actions?** The planning process is the same, but strategic planning is generally more abstract and long-range in nature while tactical plans are generally more specific and short-term. Usually an individual or group will want to determine a strategic direction and then supplemented those objectives by various tactical plans. Typically, several plans of action are happening simultaneously with most groups.

- **How much group involvement is needed?** More people involved in the planning process brings more ideas and perspectives to the process, but will require more time and effort to build consensus and aligned actions. Sometimes a smaller group is more appropriate, especially for tactical plans.

- **Who are the stakeholders in the group?** What people are likely to be affected by this plan, and who might want to have input to the direction of the group? What stakeholder are not being heard? What efforts are we making to make sure all stakeholders have input?

- **Does the group seem to have a well-defined purpose?** Many groups do not have a clear vision of their overall purpose. Individual desires and values distract them or there may be a lack of leadership defining their purpose. One of the most important products of group planning is helping establish purpose or mission for the group.

- **Who are the individuals involved in this planning process?** What personal agendas and motives might they have? What are their desires, aspirations, or fears?

- **Who is responsible for the performance of the organization?** What is their involvement in this planning process? Who is the chief decision-maker?

A leader developing a group plan needs to get adequate input from the appropriate stakeholders in the **imagining** and **goal setting** phases of planning. Determining the **current situation** and **available resources** tend to require more specialized information from subject matter experts within the organization.

For example, front-line staff may have some good ideas about the organization's customer service commitment, but the Chief Financial Officer will be needed to accurately determine the financial resources of the group. When resources are allocated and specific duties assigned, someone will need to be responsible. Remember, the planning dynamic goes from abstract ideals to concrete actions. Typically in group planning, the involvement is as inclusive as possible in the abstract phases and becomes more specialized as the process becomes more concrete.

Group planning does not have to happen in a boardroom or formalized setting. It does not need a rigid time-frame. Often a leader can use information and viewpoints collected from casual conversations and activities that do not relate directly to a formalized planning session. Regardless of the method used to construct a group plan, it will help to let people know how they have contributed the process. More participation in the process translates into more participation in doing the task required to achieve goals.

COMMON FAILURES IN GROUP PLANNING

Several factors can disturb the planning process for groups and for individuals. Common failures include:

- **Failing to dream big enough.** Imagination is the driving force in planning. Groups that fail to look beyond the current performance to envision greater achievements take away this important motivational force.

- **Setting unrealistic goals.** The opposite of failing to dream big is to set unrealistic goals. This demotivates and frustrates groups as they fail in reaching expectations.

- **Failing to see the current reality.** Groups comfortable with illusion instead of reality will never be able to maximize their effectiveness. People tend to overstate strengths and understate weaknesses.

- **Failing to allocate resources.** To undertake task leading toward goal accomplishment usually requires expending resources. Many groups frustrate themselves by stating noble goals, but failing to assign resources to achieve those goals.

- **Calling all levels of planning Strategic.** Strategic simply means long-range. Typical organizational strategic planning tends to be fairly abstract, comprehensive, broad, and general in nature. There may be a need for a multitude of planning besides "strategic planning." Operational plans, tactical plans, business plans, and other types of short-term planning require more detailed allocation of resources and action steps than an organizational strategic plan may prescribe.

- **Judging success by perception instead of performance.** One of the cornerstones of effective planning is the ability to see the current reality. Planning that relies on how the stakeholders feel about the results is likely to be ineffective. Part of the planning process should include establishing measurements of success and methods to evaluate performance.

- **Lack of diversity.** Group planning can be an arduous task. Often leaders utilize people that are like-minded to construct the group plan. This can retard the plan's ability to utilize the perspective and input from people with diverse backgrounds.

Conclusions

The planning process is ever-changing and evolving to meet the challenges of outside influences, which are also changing. The road to achieving goals can be filled with roadblocks, detours, and other barriers. Planning must be flexible to succeed, and constantly evaluating the current reality of the situation. A good plan is not necessarily a detailed blueprint of how to act and react. As General George S. Patton once said, "A good plan executed right now is far better than a perfect plan executed next week."

Planning is a tool providing purpose and importance to routine actions. It is a method of turning vague ideals, into obtainable goals while organizing the resources and actions to achieve those goals. Planning is creative and active to meet the evolving challenges and opportunities of life.

The planning dynamic is a process of determining what goals need to be pursued and how to pursue them. It is a powerful method to establish purpose, provide driving force, resolve conflicts, and direct a group. Planning is also a useful tool to provide a common vocabulary for a group—to get all of the players working in concert while creating better communication for effectiveness. Things get done without formal planning, but real accomplishments are achieved with the direction and purpose the planning process provides.

Key Points

- Challenge yourself to dream big...to imagine an ideal future.
- Objectively determine your strengths and weakness.
- Set specific, measurable, obtainable, and challenging goals with a time deadline.
- Allocate resources to close the gap between "Where you are" and "Where you want to be."
- Do the little things to accomplish the big things in life.
- Planning is a continuous process, which is constantly affecting the current situation and available resources.

PART III

Solving Problems While Managing Conflict

Problems, conflicts, and other forms of organizational distress are often symptoms that change is occurring or that change needs to happen. Leaders must be able to distinguish between symptoms and root causes of conflict. The ability to solve problems and resolve conflicts is an effective method to build influence, but sometimes leaders have to manage conflict in a way that leads to positive improvement and organizational learning.

Chapter 9
Dynamic of Problem Solving:
Building Influence and Organizational Learning

> *"A pessimist sees the problem in every opportunity;*
> *an optimist sees the opportunity in every difficulty."*
>
> Winston Churchill

When my wife and I married many years ago, we were given an old avocado green washer and dryer. Though somewhat unattractive, the washer and dryer were a much-appreciated convenience. It was much better spending time in our honeymoon cottage, than making trips to the laundromat. The washer and dryer worked fairly well…at least the washer did.

The dryer turned into a real challenge. It took a long time to dry the clothes and seemed to breakdown at least once a month. Although not particularly handy with mechanical devices, I became quite adept at tearing the old dryer down and making the necessary repairs. The drive belt and the heating element were the main problem. I kept a back-up supply and could change the parts like an Indianapolis 500 pit crew changing tires on a racecar.

Eventually, we spent more on parts to fix the old dryer than it cost to buy a new one. When we went to the store to purchase a replacement dryer, a sales clerk immediately tried to sell us a new pair of washer and dryer. I explained the washer (besides being avocado green) was in good working order. This person, however, was not just an order-taker, but a real salesperson and a problem solver.

Sales work requires good listening skills, good communication skills, and excellent problem solving ability. Being wary of all the sales tricks, I was on the defensive. I was not, however, prepared for the salesperson to help me identify the real problem. After all, I knew the problem; the dryer was a clunker.

The salesperson explained it was rare for a washer or dryer to wear out before its match. He went on to question the nature of the problem. The salesperson said dryers did not normally go through belts and heating elements the way mine was. He then asked about the washing machine. I was at first reluctant to discuss the washer because I came to replace the problem, which was the dryer. The salesperson explained how the two machines were supposed to work together, *as a system,* to clean clothes.

As I described the laundry details to him, he listened. He then asked if the washing machine was spinning properly. I answered with a confused, "What?" The salesperson went on to explain the last cycle of the wash should spin the load, taking as much of the water out of the clothes as possible before putting them in the dryer. I did not know about the spinning, but the clothes were dripping wet when they came out of the washer and into the dryer. He advised us to go home and check to see if the washer was spinning the clothes.

Knowing the right answer is rarely as valuable as knowing the right questions to ask.

Later in the afternoon, we ended up buying a new washer and a new dryer. The salesperson understood we were not just buying an appliance, but the utility or usefulness of the appliance. One of the biggest barriers in problem solving is confusing symptoms with the root cause of the real problem. For many months I had "solved the problem" of an unreliable dryer when the real problem had been the washing machine, which was not doing its job. The heavy, wet clothes were simply overworking the belt and the heating element of the dryer.

Going to the store to buy a replacement dryer was not going to solve the problem at all...it was just fixing a symptom of the problem. The old dryer may have worked for many more years if the real problem of a faulty washer had been solved first.

Problem solving requires identifying the real **problem**, listing **all** of the possible solutions, choosing the best **solution**, and **evaluating** the results of the choice. Many times problem solving is faulty for the same reason the problem solving failed in fixing the old dryer. To solve a problem, you must first identify what the real problem is!

Problems can be sporadic or chronic, big or small, tactical or strategic. The ability to effectively solve problems requires expertise in decision-making and observation. Effective problem solving becomes a tool to help a leader build influence by demonstrating their competence.

Sporadic problems tend to be random, single situations, which are dealt with one time. A flat tire, though inconvenient, is usually an infrequent occurrence. Chronic problems are more continuous situations and usually more serious. For a company, a lost check can be a problem, which is sporadic or temporary in nature while the company's inability to meet its financial obligations may be a chronic, longer-term problem, which will continue if action is not taken. Sporadic problems will sometimes go away, but chronic problems are here to stay unless solved.

Dynamic of Problem Solving
The P.A.S.E. Method

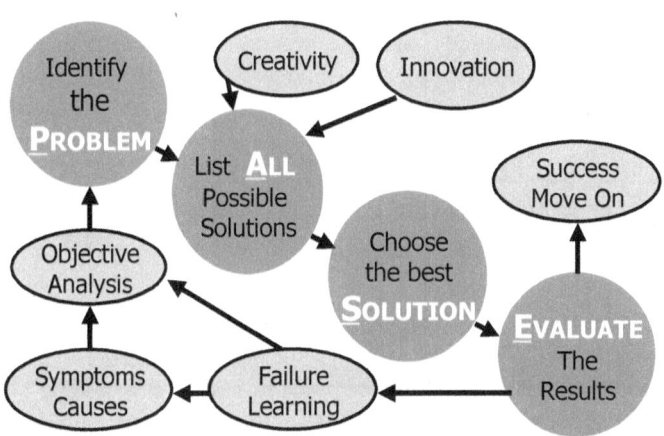

The P.A.S.E. problem solving formula is comprised of identifying the **PROBLEM**, listing **ALL** of the possible solutions, choosing the best **SOLUTION**, and then **EVALUATING** the results. This model of solving problems is an effective methodology for resolving sporadic, simple, and technical problems. The model works well on problems needing a technical fix, but the key is in the first step, identifying the problem.

Properly identifying the **PROBLEM** is essential to finding a solution. Many times separating the symptoms from the problem can be confusing. Someone experiencing an upper respiratory infection may experience congestion, minor aches, sore throat, and coughing. There are various over-the-counter medicines, which will temporarily relieve these symptoms. Unfortunately, treating the symptoms and making them "feel" better does not always solve the problem. The person may need rest and time for their immune system to fight the infection. If the infection is severe, they may need antibiotics or other treatment to solve the problem and get rid of the infection. Failure to properly treat the infection or the real problem can lead to serious future health concerns.

Dealing with chronic problems requires identifying the root causes of the problem. Being objective and non-biased is important in successfully analyzing problems and their causes. Identifying the problem should involve the gathering of data, facts, and careful, objective analysis to determine the reality of the situation. Having the vision to see things for what they really are instead of how we think they are is essential in identifying a problem.

Problems involving personal relationships and conflicts are particularly difficult to see objectively. Emotions, opinions, and preconceived ideas can be strong influences affecting the attitude toward a person. In conflict situations occurring between groups, **polarized paranoia** cripples the ability to see things objectively and to determine what the real problems are. Polarized paranoia happens when groups within an organization have the perception others are either all evil or all good.

American politics are an example of polarized paranoia. Individuals are perceived as being villainous or heroic depending on which side is talking about them. In reality, few people are all right or all wrong. All people have strengths and weaknesses, good ideas and some brainless ones. The challenge is to see beyond the preconceived ideas, strong personal opinions, and emotions to find truth.

Organizations often suffer from this phenomenon of polarized paranoia. Individuals or groups become singled out as the opposition, clouding the ability of people to see things for what they really are. Many times a person becomes the scapegoat and problems are blamed on them while the real causes remain invisible. Sometimes individuals, particularly destructive attitude people **(See Chapter 13, Dynamic of Character)**, are the cause of the problems. Good problem solvers focus on the specific actions, issue, and reality. They are able to look past the personalities and people to see the truth in a situation.

Effectively identifying problems and root causes involve the same skills used to create a vision of the current reality. **(See Chapter 2, Dynamic of Vision)** Collecting data, searching for facts, becoming non-emotional, analyzing the driving force and controlling force, and listening to different perspectives can help identify the root causes to problems to make better problem solving decisions. Answering the all-important question *why* **(See Chapter 6, Dynamic of Purpose)** is essential in identifying root causes.

After the problem and root causes have been identified, the problem-solver needs to list **ALL** the possible solutions. Having the self-confidence to be innovative and creative can help in finding all of the possible solutions. Some of the most workable plans or solutions may be the most simple and obvious. Being creative and innovative can help in problem solving, but it is also important to not overlook obvious solutions.

After all of the possible solutions have been analyzed, choose the best **SOLUTION** and be confident in the fact, given all of the possible solutions, the best one has been chosen. Self-assured people are able to take responsibility for problem solving decisions. They also understand the nature of problem solving sometimes means failure or further challenges.

After a solution has been chosen, effective problem solvers will **EVALUATE** the results. In evaluating the effectiveness and success of a solution, the problem solver needs a learning attitude. Problem solvers need to be willing to learn from failure and make better decisions in the future.

Limitations of Problem Solving

An old English proverb says, "A smooth sea never made a skilled sailor." Few people enjoy trials and tribulations, but problems and conflict can be indicative of change or the need for positive improvement. It is not always possible to solve problems with a quick methodology or system. Although some situations can be fixed by short-range decision-making, many problems take more time, and require people to adapt their behaviors, attitudes, and even beliefs. One fundamental flaw societies, governments, business organizations, and individuals make is trying to solve complex problems with simple solutions. Problem solving is an effective and useful skill for a leader to provide safety to the group and build influence, but solving short-term, technical problems has limitations.

Micro versus Macro

One limitation to problem solving is the relationship between micro problems compared to macro problems. Micro simply means small and is used as a prefix to modify numerous words. For example, micro-economics is concerned with how basic economic principles apply and affect individual entities, while macro-economics looks at the effects of the same economic principles on industries, nations, and even world economies. The basic principles are similar but the focus and perspective is radically different.

Effective problem solvers must determine if they are dealing with micro-situations or macro-situations. Our tendency is to think in isolation and assume most issues are micro-issues when, in fact, many challenging situations are interconnected and have a macro-implication. Solutions applied in isolation may have an adverse effect to the macro system.

For example, a city does a detailed study of crime rates and determine the most crime occur in a two-block area close to downtown. The micro solution involves sending more patrols through, installing security cameras, and making sure property is secure. These solutions may work in the two-block area, but the crime may simply spreads to other parts of the city creating new challenge. A macro solution to the problem might require examining other factors such as the neighborhood socio-economic dynamics. Is there a lack of educational opportunities? Is there a poverty issue? Could the adding better lighting have the same effect as increased police presence? Tackling macro problems can be complex and take extended time, but overreacting with micro solutions can lead to unintended consequences that create problems that are more challenging in the future.

Technical Solutions versus Adaptive Challenges

Technical solutions can solve problems that require short-term actions or decisions to correct something that is not working as designed. Technical solutions might fix a short-term dilemma, but sometimes there are not easy answers or solutions to a conflict. Occasionally a group needs to adapt to meet new challenges. Adaptive challenges require different and more subtle leadership skills because they involve changing the attitudes, behaviors, culture, or even the beliefs of a group. Using technical solutions to treat adaptive challenge situations are like treating the symptoms while ignoring the disease.

With technical solutions, the leader may be able to provide the decision-making and problems solving. They identify the **problem**, list **all** the possible solution, chose the best **solution**, and **evaluate** the results. In adaptive challenges, the burden of the work transfers from the expert or leader to the followers. The leader's role is often to interpret the symptoms, identify the root causes of the conflict, and set parameters or controlling forces to facilitate the new skills needed to adapt to the new challenges. People may have to change behaviors, attitudes, or beliefs to survive the new challenges.

For example, a patient goes to the doctor complaining of pain. The doctor (the expert) may be able to diagnosis the problem by analyzing the symptoms and prescribe a treatment based on this diagnosis. A simple pain reliever and anti-inflammatory drug might solve the problem. The doctor has supplied a technical solution to a short-term health problem. Everyone is looking for this fix when going to the doctor. I don't feel well. The doctor gave me something. Now I feel good. Sometimes, however, the doctor will evaluate the symptoms and find there are no technical fixes or easy answers. The solution may require complicated procedures or require a patient to *change behaviors*. Sometimes a simple technical solution will not work.

Many health problems are behavioral. The National Institute of Health reported that, "If we could get Americans to do just three things, stop smoking, stop drinking alcohol, and stop being obese, we could eliminate over 87% of all diseases in the United States."[8] Health problems related to lifestyle choices often require more than a technical or simple solution. The patient may have to modify their behavior, change diet, or develop an exercise routine. Any prescription the doctor might make would only relieve symptoms if the root cause involves behavior or lifestyle. Facing an adaptive challenge, the doctor's role evolves from problem solver to a teacher as he or she prepares the patient for their new reality.

---

[8] National Institute of Health web page, www.nih.gov, 2004.

Some Solutions Cause New Problems

Several years ago, I was invited to speak at a conference. The day or two before the event, I developed a sinus condition with a stuffing nose, a cough, and sore throat. Not wanting to cancel at the last minute, I took heavy doses of over-the-counter antihistamine so I could breathe and talk. The medication worked well and by the time I began the presentation, I could breathe, was not coughing, and even felt like my voice was fairly clear.

Problem solved—or so I thought. About 15 minutes into the presentation, my mouth got dry. I drank a glass of water. Talked a some more and then drank more water. I had never been so thirsty in my life. Eventually I had to have the event coordinator bring me a pitcher of water, which I drank. Solving the problem of the stuffy nose and congestion caused an entirely new problem of an extremely dry mouth and the need to drink vast quantities of water. Drinking a large amount of water created yet another problem when I had to stand in a reception line and greet the audience after the presentation!

Many times, solutions to our short-term problems lead to bigger and more complex future problems. A manufacturing company solves a bottleneck in their production process, which gives the sales force much more product to sell than had been anticipated. This causes inventories to swell and puts pressure on the sales force to sell the overages. The sales manager decides the only way to sell that much product is to discount the price, which solves the problems of the excess inventory, but hurts the company's profits. Since many issues are interconnected or macro problems the solutions can create new and more serious challenges when people think in isolation or look only at the micro problem.

Time and Space

Life is about making choices, about the consequences and rewards of those choices. The difficulty in making the right choices in problem solving is that effects and causes are not always close in time or space.

My first driver's license at age 16 recorded my height as 5'10", my eyes as being green, and my weight as 135 pounds. A trip to the doctor's office at age 42 revealed that the height was still 5"10", the eyes were still green, but the weight was a hefty 228 pounds. I had transformed from a too skinny teenager to a too plumb adult.

This transformation happened over a 25-year period by decisions made in eating and exercise (or the lack of it.)

One of the challenges in reforming these eating and exercise habits was that the effects of the choices were not close in time. Occasionally I would overeat and have heartburn for a short period of time and my waist size had increased an inch or two every couple of years, but eating what I wanted tasted good and made me feel (at least in the short-term) satisfied. The lack of exercise also had no immediate consequences. In fact, refraining from exercise resulted in no heavy breathing, no sore muscles, and very little sweat. In the micro perspective overeating and under exercising presented no consequences but even seemed to have rewards.

The doctor, however, burst my bubble by explaining the consequences of eating what I wanted, when I wanted, while not exercising. A man my age, he explained, needed to eat a balanced diet and exercise regularly. The consequences, he continued, might include future heart problems, diabetes, a shorter life, and most certainly a poorer quality of life. The consequences for over eating and under exercising were sure although they were taking decades to be revealed. The doctor convinced me to make changes, alter my eating habits, and begin exercising. I did lose my weight and got down to a trim 175 pounds. I felt great. So great that I fell back into old habits and trip to the doctor at age 55 showed me at 205 pounds and needing to make changes again.

Dieting and getting into an exercise routine had its own challenges. Exercising is uncomfortable and worst of all the daily trips to the scales shows the weight was not coming off very fast. Unfortunately, it takes much less time to get out of shape than to get back into shape.

Problems are rarely static, but instead are dynamic and constantly presenting new challenges. Trying to apply short-term, technical fixes to perceived micro problems can limit the abilities of a person or group to effectively deal with longer-term adaptive challenge that require looking at the macro perspective.

Problem Solving in Leadership

Leaders are faced with many challenges and one of the most common is problem solving. It is not necessary for the leader to solve every problem. Sometimes the leader needs to develop the people in the group by empowering them to solve their own problems. Effective leaders should be teaching others how to solve problems. The P.A.S.E. methodology can be an excellent tool to help others understand the nature of problem solving.

Sometimes it is necessary for the leader to step in and solve the problem. In times of crisis or distress, followers depend on leaders who can solve problems, provide safety, and maintain a stable environment. Leaders who become confident and competent in using the problem-solving dynamic are well equipped to provide this safety and stability. The ability to solve the group's problems and provide security to the group is also an effective method to demonstrate competence by the leader and build influence.

Leaders solve problems by analyzing the situation and looking beyond the symptoms to identify the real problem. They are innovative and creative in listing all of the possible solutions, taking care not to overlook obvious and easy solutions. Leaders then take responsibility to choose and implement a solution. Leaders with the best instincts for leading know how to evaluate the results of the decision and make further adjustments.

Good leaders do not fear failure, but instead look at problems as learning opportunities. If the solution does not work, they take responsibility. If the solution does work, they are quick to share the credit. Leaders do not dread problems. They look at them as opportunities and challenges to prove excellence. Leaders do not worry about problems; they solve them and learn from them.

High levels of self-assurance are helpful in being innovative and creative during problem solving. The ability to be objective and see the reality of situations helps in identifying the real problems instead of the superficial symptoms. Taking responsibility for decisions and maintaining an attitude of learning in spite of failure are true measures of an expert problem solver.

Key Points

- Identifying the real problem instead of symptoms is a key element in developing problem-solving ability.
- Polarized Paranoia is a barrier to solving problems involving people and groups of people. Learning to focus on the specific situation and real issues instead of the personalities involved can help solve problems.
- The **P.A.S.E.** problem-solving model involves identifying the real **PROBLEM**, listing **ALL** the possible solutions, choosing the best **SOLUTION**, and **EVALUTATING** the results.
- There are some limitations to Problem Solving
    - o   Micro versus Macro problems
    - o   Technical Problems versus Adaptive Challenges
    - o   Some solutions create new problems
    - o   Time and space
- Problems and conflicts are often symptoms that change is occurring or needs to occur.

Chapter 10
Dynamic of Conflict:
Controlling the Creative Energy of Conflict for Organizational Results

> *"Difficulties are meant to rouse, not discourage.*
> *The human spirit is to grow strong by conflict."*
>
> William Ellery Channing

Conflict is an inevitable occurrence in interpersonal relationships. The word conflict originates from the Latin word *"conflictus"* which literally means the act of striking together. A variety of influences and factors cause conflict. Most conflict occurs when the goals of an individual or group becomes a barrier to the goals and desires of others. Understanding, managing, and even using conflict for constructive improvement is essential in leadership.

CONFLICT ≠ CONTEST

Conflict is generally perceived as a negative occurrence, but conflict is not inherently good or bad. Conflict does not necessarily equal a contest. In a contest, one side wins and the other loses. Many times in managing conflict, it is important to see that both sides either win or lose equally.

Though most people do not enjoy conflict, it has some positive effects. Conflict can energize and motivate people. It can be a stimulus for change and a source for improvement. Competition, a mild form of conflict, can be a tremendous motivator. However, competition can lead to wasted effort and inefficiency when a group is unsure of its overall mission and purpose.

When properly handled, conflict leads to problem solving, personal growth, and learning. Conflict, like problems, is often a symptom indicating more serious issues, which need to be corrected. Ignoring conflict and not seeing it as a symptom to bigger problems and challenges, can lead to disastrous consequences.

Conflict can energize and motivate people toward positive problem solving and constructive change. It often signals an opportunity for change and improvement. Conflict when handled with an attitude of **learning instead of competing**, improves interpersonal relationships. The ability to admit and learn from mistakes is a powerful method to resolve conflict and build influential communications.

Negative Consequences of Unresolved Conflict

Unresolved conflict often escalates into destructive and even volatile situations. Conflict becomes negative when it causes frustration and leads to lost productivity, personal stress, or even violence. Stress is a physical and mental state of not being able to handle the emotions of a circumstance while violence can involve physical actions against others.

Many times individuals avoid conflict by substituting productive tasks with easier and less confrontational activities.

There can be a variety of negative reactions to conflict. Negative consequences do not always originate with the conflict but rather with the inability to effectively deal with conflict. Many times individuals avoid conflict by substituting productive tasks with easier and less confrontational activities. A person's fear of conflict and confrontation can become a barrier to developing an assertive and open communication style. Rather than expressing themselves, they passively avoid sharing their ideas and opinions to avoid any possible conflict.

Lessons from Lincoln

Unresolved conflicts will not go away and may result in even greater future difficulties. The issue of slavery had been a boiling caldron of controversy in the United States since the nation's independence from Britain. The issue was avoided and compromised for about eighty years before armed conflict broke out. The Missouri Compromise of 1820 and the Compromise of

1850 delayed the inevitable conflict. It was easier to address the organization of new territories than the current realities of the existing states. The Kansas Nebraska Act of 1854 finally motivated the creation of the Republican Party, which overtly opposed slavery and its extension into new territories.

Conflict presents opportunities for leaders who can focus attention on problems and take action toward moving to solutions. Ignoring conflict or focusing on the symptoms instead of the real causes can be catastrophic. James Buchanan, who won the presidential election in 1854, dealt with the conflicts brewing in the country by ignoring them and keeping the status quo. By the time Abraham Lincoln took office in 1860, he faced irreconcilable differences and conflict between proponents of slavery and abolitionists.

Lincoln was an immensely unpopular president both north and south through most of his four-year term. He was forced to make hard and unpopular choices while facing the highest degree of conflict...war. Lincoln did not cause the war by himself; he simply had to deal with conflicts previous generations avoided. Lincoln is considered one of our greatest presidents for his ability to lead a nation through conflict to new hopes of national excellence.

Avoiding conflict may sometimes seem the easy course, but avoidance may be destructive instead of constructive to the group. Some people when faced with conflict become excessively negative or cynical about everything and everyone in the organization. This negativism is another avoidance mechanism in dealing with the barriers and problems of the conflict.

Dealing with conflict is a valuable skill that can build a leader's influence.

People have a keen ability to rationalize or make excuses for not handling conflict. They may choose to ignore conflict or develop an attitude of indifference. Some may blame others to compensate for their lack of ability to deal with the conflict. Effectively dealing with conflict requires accepting responsibility for identifying, analyzing, and solving the root causes of the conflict. Many times avoiding or procrastinating action causes more stress than the actual conflict.

Types of Conflict

Conflict can be intra-personal, interpersonal, or structural in nature. **Intra-personal conflict** involves conflicts an individual has with their own decision-making. Different personality types, poor communication, rivalry, and competition cause **interpersonal conflicts**. **Structural conflict** occurs when individuals or groups are competing for scarce resources, when goals are differentiated, when people are dependent on others, when the lines of responsibility are not clearly defined, or when communication breaks down.

Intra-personal conflict happens when a person is in conflict with himself or herself. There are a variety of factors, which cause intra-personal conflict and anxiety. Many people are at conflict with themselves because their actions are not congruent with their beliefs or their goals. Sometimes a person has a personal conflict because they must choose between two or more positive alternatives. In economics this is known as "opportunity cost" meaning something must be given up to obtain something else. The old saying, "You can't have your cake and eat it to," would be like choosing between two desirable activities.

Often a person must choose between two or more negative alternatives. "Caught between a rock and a hard place," describes a conflict situation many people face at some point in their life. Sometimes tough choices must be made, which are not popular. Abraham Lincoln had the choice of preserving the Union or letting the Southern states leave the United States. His decision to defend federal property in the South, after those states had politically left the Union, was a bloody and painful one. The alternative was to divide the country in two and leave approximately 3.9 million people in slavery.

Supervision in many organizations often becomes one of the most stressful jobs because the nature of the position deals with conflict. Supervisors are constantly caught in the middle, between the people they supervise and work with, and decision-makers in upper management. Many times, supervisors have to carry out the policies of the organization when they may have had little input in those decisions. Supervisors also have to do employee evaluations and observations. One of the challenges of supervision is to write honest, constructive, and accurate descriptions of work performance. Supervisors often have the tendency to "sugar-coat" evaluations to avoid the conflict or telling the employee they are not doing a good job. The conflict of telling the truth in a tactful way or ignoring a circumstance is a type of intra-personal conflict.

Doing the right thing is not always easy, but it is always the right thing to do. However, doing the right thing does not always relieve the stress and conflict in a situation. Consequences are

Doing the right thing is not always easy, but it is always the right thing to do.

the result of making choices. Avoidance occurs when situations are so stressful the individual dodges an activity or responsibility, which might otherwise be beneficial in obtaining goals.

Interpersonal conflicts originate from personality and differing values, including socio and economic diversity. Different personalities and character types relate positively or negatively to other people. A person's communication style, values, beliefs, ethics, morals, and competition become other factors in interpersonal conflicts.

Self-assurance and a healthy self-image are the foundation to successful character development. Self-assured individuals can better accept other peoples' ideas and opinions. They are better equipped to listen, admit mistakes, and change than people who have low self-confidence. Assured people do not feel threatened by the diversity of other people. They do not feel they have to compete and win the contest of ideas and opinions. Self-confident people understand the value of others and the opportunity they have to learn from others with different experiences.

Many conflicts are blamed on interpersonal or personality differences between people. However, true interpersonal conflicts in organizations are rare. Sometimes interpersonal conflicts are actually intra-personal conflicts, which keep people from accepting the ideas of others. Often interpersonal or personality differences are masking the most common type of organizational conflict...structural conflict.

Structural conflicts arise from the way people, departments, or job responsibilities have to relate with one another. The word structural means, "The way things are built." Structural conflicts are often caused by competition over scarce resources, competitive reward systems, interdependence between work units, power differentials, and ambiguity over responsibilities.

Structural conflict can be addressed effectively, if the true nature and dynamic of the conflict is understood. Many times people assume personalities or the actions of people are causing all of the conflict. Polarized paranoia occurs when people think groups of people or individuals are either all good or all bad. I tend to believe most conflicts within organizations (even those generally identified as "personality conflicts") are structural in nature. Learning a methodology to resolve structural conflicts can help bring peace to your work group and build your personal influence.

CAUSES OF STRUCTURAL CONFLICT

Competing for Scarce Resources

The most common type of structural conflict occurs when individuals or groups compete over scarce resources. This type of conflict gets confused with personality conflicts because people working together in groups have a difficult time separating individuals from situations. For example, in an educational setting there may be many people wanting to use classroom space, laboratory space, computer time, or other scarce resources. When too many people want to use a scarce resource, a decision will be made that will not make everyone happy, and may well make no one happy. With these decisions, the parties who feel they have not gotten their fair share displace their frustration onto the group perceived as using the resource or getting their way instead of the fundamental problem of scarcity.

Competition over scarce resources not only happens with tangible assets, but also with intangible resources. There may be competition about ideas, philosophy, or who will hold influence. There may also be competition for the attention of a superior or decision maker. Competition can be a powerful motivator, but competition over scarce resources causes jealousy, stress, and conflict.

Goal Differentiation

Goal differentiation represents another common structural conflict in many groups. For example, a sales and marketing department, rewarded by units shipped, may have a different goal than the shipping department who have an incentive to reduce costs. The sales department focuses on providing product to the customer in a timely and convenient manner. However, the truck drivers and shipping people strive to keep cost down by only shipping when trucks are full. The truck drivers' motivation is not necessarily the number of units shipped or the speed with which they are shipped, but by how efficiently they ship full trucks. The sales people dealing directly with customers, who are waiting for orders not yet shipped, may see the shipping people as the problem when the conflict is actually the different goals the two departments have. To resolve this type of conflict, it is necessary to identify the source of the true conflict and create a common goal for the entire organization.

Dependence

Structural conflict also happens when individuals are dependent and rely on others in the organization, especially when the dependence is not equal. In the before mentioned case of the sales people and shipping department, this may be another cause of conflict.

Let's say the sales people are reliant on the shipping department to deliver goods. The shipping department, however, is expected to deliver the goods in an economical way. The sales people cannot complete their orders or be paid their commission until the products are shipped. The shipping people, however, are salaried. The shipping department might have raw materials to move and other divisions in the company to service. The shipping department may ultimately rely on the sales department to produce revenue, but this reliance is indirect and may not be very apparent to many of the salaried workers on the shipping dock. Goal differentiation and dependence on others are two common causes of structural conflict.

Authority and Responsibility

Imbalance in authority and responsibility is another type of structural conflict. This structural conflict is so common and destructive that an entire chapter has been devoted to analyzing its effects. **(See Chapter 11, Dynamic of Authority and Responsibility)** When responsibility and authority are not equal, chaos and stress occur. Responsibility without authority or authority without responsibility is going to be a bad situation for someone. Properly identifying the source of conflict is an essential element to leadership in an organization. Recognizing imbalances of authority and responsibility is a good start.

Poor Communication

Another structural cause of stress in an organization is poor communication. Information flows through an organization and the organization must have systems and the organizational integrity to manage this stream of information. Too much or too little information getting to individuals in the group is certain to cause conflict. **(See Chapter 15, Dynamic of Communication)** Gossiping and the rumor mill cripple many organizations. Solomon said, "For lack of wood the fire goes out: and where there is no whisper, quarreling ceases. As charcoal to hot embers and wood to fire, so is a quarrelsome man for kindling strife."[9]

Dealing with Reality

Some conflicts are caused by gaps between perception and reality. Anytime individuals or groups are forced to deal with these realities, conflict is likely.

Courts of law are stressful places full of conflict. Attorneys working in these courts are often some of the most ostracized professional people in our society. The reason attorneys are so disliked is that they have the job of dealing with this gap between peoples' perception and reality. Think about it. Two parties come to a court of law with two completely different views of reality. Both generally believe they are right because they are basing their beliefs on opinions and a skewed perspective. Attorneys ask questions and cross-examine witnesses attempting to establish truths. They present evidence that is non-biased and factual. It is no wonder attorneys have the reputation they have—they make people deal with reality and that is always and stressful situation.

Most organizational conflicts are structural in nature. Many of these conflicts are difficult to diagnose since human emotions, opinions, and perspectives are involved. Structural conflict can many times be resolved when the root causes of the conflict are properly identified. Using a systematic approach of identifying the type of conflict and then applying a well thought out solution can increase your ability to manage conflict.

---

[9] Proverbs Chapter 26 Verses 20-21, Revised Standard Version

CONFLICT MANAGEMENT STRATEGIES

Resolving conflict requires ability to properly identify the type and nature of the conflict as well as its root causes. If the conflict is structural, many methods can be employed to reduce the stress depending on the specific situation.

Use of Authority: Using legitimate power and authority to resolve a situation among individuals is perhaps the easiest solution to a simple conflict situation. A leader can simply prescribe a solution and dictate actions. This solution, however, usually works with immature groups and does little to develop the leadership capacity within an organization. Using authority to solve problems too often results in the leader becoming a surrogate parent for the group— refereeing every little dispute because the followers have not learned how to identify and manage conflict on their own.

Expand Resources: Structural conflict often revolves around competition for resources. Increasing the availability of resources to make them less scarce can reduce the tension among groups and individuals. Unfortunately, resources are usually scarce and this strategy of conflict resolution has obvious limits.

Reduce Interaction: If certain groups tend to be overly competitive with scarce resources, looking for ways to eliminate interaction between individuals and departments may be a solution. Moving the conflicting parties away from each other can bring peace, but does not really deal with the deeper sources of the conflict.

Clarifying Job Responsibilities: Making responsibilities more explicit, and identifying job duties more clearly, can help in reducing conflicts arising from responsibility differentiation and dependence on others.

Using Data and Facts: Many structural and interpersonal conflicts happen because people confuse their opinion with truth. Anytime a group of people are discussing issues based on the "I think, I feel, or I believe" conversation, conflict is likely. One of the most effective conflict resolution strategies is to pull the group back to data and facts. Make participants document points-of-view and many structural conflicts will evaporate.

Reducing Interdependence: Looking for ways to make departments and people less dependent, or at least equally dependent on each other, can help reduce conflicts between groups that perhaps have different priorities while using the same resources.

Creating Purpose and Setting Goals: One of the ways leaders can reduce internal conflicts is by creating focus on the purpose and mission of the group. This can be accomplished by focusing the group's attention on specific, clear, and measurable goals.

Create Integrators: Developing people in the organization that can liaison between departments and individuals can be an asset. The ability to deal effectively with people is always useful. One of the most valuable skills in the workplace and in life is the ability to network people, groups, and ideas together. Leaders should always be looking for or creating common denominators between groups and individuals.

Negotiation: Negotiation is a communication strategy that looks for win-win opportunities, or at least fair ways to resolve conflicts. Negotiators resolve conflict by adhering to the principle that everyone must win or lose as equally as possible, and if it's not a good deal for everyone, it's not a good deal for anyone.

Balance Authority and Responsibility: Ensuring people have adequate amounts of authority for the responsibility they have reduces stress. Making sure individuals are not taking authority without taking responsibility will help eliminate chaos in the organization.

Elimination: Sometimes barriers causing the conflict must be removed or eliminated. These barriers can include outdated ideas or beliefs, space, communication systems, inefficient processes or other assets. Sometimes it is even necessary to eliminate individuals from the group that are disruptive and unwilling to change and improve.

RESOLVING DESTRUCTIVE CONFLICTS

One of the biggest barriers to leadership is the lack of vision for the current reality. This lack of vision is also one of the challenges in dealing with conflict. The leader must be able to see situations for what they are, make non-emotional decisions, and take responsibility for the consequences. Resolving conflicts is rarely easy or neat. A leader must have patience and foresight to make the hard decisions, and the diligence to guide the group toward positive improvement and change.

If a conflict escalates, it can become a confrontation. Effectively dealing with confrontational situations can provide safety and stability to a group and increase the leader's level of influence. When conflict evolves into confrontation, the leader is past taking preventative, proactive, or constructive actions to resolve the conflict. Facing confrontation becomes an emergency. Survival, limiting destruction, and protecting the group is the goal in resolving these severe conflicts.

In a confrontational situation, the leader should attempt to defuse the conflict or at least defer the conflict to a more opportune time. When faced with an emotional situation:

1. **Don't react...listen.** Angry people are not in an emotional state to have a rational discussion. When agitated, people need to be given the opportunity to vent their anger and frustration. When people are venting their anger, it is important to be mature and self-assured enough to know the person is not demeaning you, they are just angry. Responding to their anger will only add fuel to the flame.

2. **Deal with the situation not the personalities.** Encourage the person to focus on "what" has happened instead of "who" is involved.

3. After the person has vented their anger and become less emotional, try to **identify the existing problem and possible causes.**

4. **Ask the other person to suggest possible solutions** .When possible, let the other person talk and brainstorm possible solutions. After all, people will generally agree with themselves. When confronted by anger, be rational and try to limit emotional responses.

5. **Look for areas of agreement** and opportunities to give options and choices instead of directives or orders.

6. **Focusing on the situation and not the people** involved is one way of reducing the level of emotional fog clouding many conflict situations.

7. **Look for practical alternatives** and common denominators or interest to open up communication. Open communication **(See Chapter 15, Dynamic of Communication)** where individuals have a high curiosity for the truth, a high level of concern for other people, and an ability to positively influence others, is the best tool in effectively dealing with conflict.

8. **Try to give options and choices instead of directives and instructions.** Agitated people are not in a state of mind to take directives. They can resist even the most sensible suggestions. Giving them options, even if the choices are similar, can start a more constructive conversation.

Conflict does not have to equal a contest. Conflicts are opportunities to see what the real issues are and make positive improvements, which will not only eliminate future conflicts, but improve the group's capacity to adapt and grow.

Key Points

- Conflict does not equal Contest.
- Deal with the situation instead of the personalities.
- Conflict can be Intra-personal, Interpersonal, or Structural.
- Identify the type of conflict then chose an appropriate strategy.
- To defuse confrontation:
    1. Don't react…Listen.
    2. Let people vent anger…express empathy.
    3. Identify the real problem…not the symptom.
    4. Ask the other person to suggest possible solutions.
    5. Try to give options and choices instead of directives and instructions.

Chapter 11
Dynamic of
Authority and Responsibility:
Balancing a Group toward Productivity

"He that will not apply new remedies must expect new evils;
for time is the greatest innovator."

Francis Bacon

Imbalance of authority and responsibility causes damaging structural conflict in a group. Developing the ability to analyze and keep these two factors in equilibrium will help in resolving conflict and maximizing the capacity for success for a group.

Lee, Stonewall, and Ewell

In May of 1863, Robert E. Lee won perhaps the most impressive victory of the American Civil War at Chancellorsville, Virginia. Facing an army two and half times as large as his own and better equipped in every way, Lee sent his best general, Stonewall Jackson, on a daring maneuver through the woods to flank and rout the Federal army. Lee said of Jackson, "I had such implicit confidence in Jackson's skill and energy that I never troubled myself to give him detailed instruction. The most general suggestions were all that he needed."[10]

Jackson, however, died in the attack. Lee replaced him with General R. S. Ewell. Ewell had served under Jackson but Lee had little interaction with him while he was on Jackson's staff. Some who had served with Ewell were aware he did not feel comfortable initiating a plan unless he received input and support from others. Lee never had an opportunity to discover this lack of self-confidence Ewell had in himself, nor was Lee aware Ewell's

---

[10] Freeman, Douglas S, R. E. Lee A Biography, Volume III, page 1, 1940, Charles Scribner's Sons, New York

experiences with Jackson trained him to obey the letter of an orders and not to exercise discretion.[11]

Three months after Lee's dramatic victory at Chancellorsville, he suffered his biggest defeat in the Pennsylvania town of Gettysburg. Lee arrived in Gettysburg on July 1, 1863, in perfect position. Lee saw the high ground on this battlefield was just south of Gettysburg on Culp's Hill. Lee knew his troops had an opportunity so he issued Ewell "discretionary orders" which he was accustomed to doing when Jackson was in command. He wanted Ewell to press the attack and take Culp's Hill. Lee had given the same order to Jackson many times… "There's the hill, take it. I don't care how. You have the authority and responsibility to do the job." Unfortunately for Lee, Ewell was not Jackson, and he did not react the way Jackson would have.

Ewell arrived at the hill in good position but waited for further, more detailed instructions from Lee. Ewell reacted indecisively. Lee's discretionary instructions confused Ewell, who was accustomed to the more explicit orders he always received from Jackson. He complained at the time of Lee's vague directions. Ewell was passive and indecisive at a critical time in the battle while waiting further orders from Lee. The differences between Ewell, who needed explicit instructions, and Jackson, who thrived on general directives, were drastic. One staff officer from Stonewall Jackson's army stated, "Jackson is not here!"

Jackson had been a member of Lee's command who had been given high levels of authority to accomplish a task. Ewell was a person who was more comfortable following explicit instructions. When authority was given to him as it had been to Jackson, he was not prepared for it. Robert E. Lee's military loss at Gettysburg was partly caused by failing to realize how the dynamic of authority and responsibility work.

With authority comes responsibility and with responsibility comes authority. Leaders must be able to balance these two functions for people in an organization to work harmoniously and productively. Authority without responsibility and responsibility without authority are bad situations for someone. This dynamic causes stress and chaos when there is not a balance between the

---

[11] Freeman, Douglas S., R.E. Lee A Biography, Volume III, page 11, 1940, Charles Scribner's Sons, New York

two. General Jackson had been the kind of soldier who was willing to take great responsibility and was given equal authority to carry out the task. Ewell had been given the authority, but did not use it and did not want the level of responsibility, which had been given Jackson. Disaster for Lee was the result.

Routine—Controlled

Jobs assigning minimal authority and requiring little responsibility are described as routine. These duties are typically very controlled, leaving the individual a small scope of decision-making. Routine work is necessary and can be productive, but the level of responsibility must balance the level of authority.

Dynamic of Authority/Responsibility

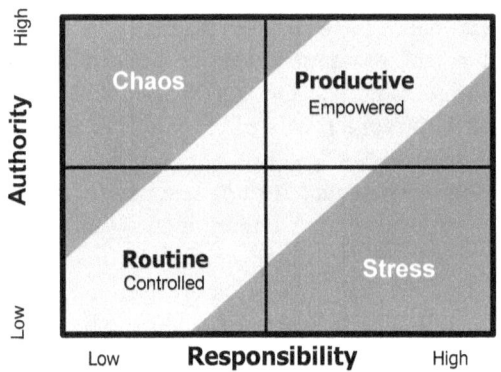

Many people are task-oriented with an aptitude for routine work. They do not like the pressure of making decisions or the added responsibility. Entry-level jobs and tasks, which are repetitive, are most likely to be routine. The fry cook at a fast food restaurant or a private in the military are examples of routine work. Anytime someone is given low authority to make decisions and little responsibility for overall group effectiveness, that person is doing routine work.

Although routine work does not cause much stress or chaos, the need for routine jobs is declining in the modern workplace. Some people will be content to work at this level, but the chance for advancement and the ability to add value to the group is restricted in routine work. Most organizations need to develop people who are more productive and empowered to take responsibility. These organizations must balance the empowerment of authority to make decisions with the person's ability to assume more responsibility. This process of development may include periods of stress and slight chaos as individuals take on more responsibility and authority.

Chaos

In many organizations, the dynamic of authority and responsibility is out of balance causing lost productivity and chaos. When individuals in a group are exerting excessive authority without taking an equal amount of responsibility, the group is likely to experience chaos. Many organizations exist with some level of chaos when people misuse authority. Individuals taking authority while failing to take responsibility can be destructive to a group.

Organizational chaos often happens when subordinate members of a group assume authority while not taking an equal measure of responsibility. Destructive people **(See Chapter 13, Dynamic of Character)** will often criticize and second guess activities for which they are not responsible. Many times this criticism happens when they do not know all of the facts. When the authority of leadership is undermined by individuals usurping authority, it weakens the organizational structure and makes it more difficult for the group to make anyone responsible. Destructive people like this type of chaos. When these "captains of chaos" are able to disrupt the organization, it takes the focus off their activities and their unwillingness to take responsibility for their actions.

Chaos occurs in groups when people take authority without taking responsibility, but it also happens when those who are given the responsibility fail to accept it. The chaos is even worse when a person in authority fails to accept responsibility by always blaming others. This situation causes bad morale, fear, and suspicion as well as chaos. Being the leader is more than a title. Leaders take responsibility, but also share credit for success.

Whenever someone is taking authority and not taking the equal amount of responsibility, chaos happens. The chaos caused by people taking too much authority and too little responsibility sometimes manifest itself in the form of a superior who second guesses, micro-manages, or unfairly places blame on others. People become cautious, bewildered, and stagnate when leaders fail to take appropriate responsibility. Leadership involves responsibility...even the responsibility for other people. A leader's creed should be:

If things go well, you did it.

If things go okay, we did it.

If things go badly, I did it.

When leaders demonstrate responsibility, they are taking the first step in empowering the people around them to take higher levels of authority and responsibility.

Stress

Stress is common in many groups, and a variety of factors cause the tension and strain it puts on organizations. One of the chief causes, however, is the dynamic of authority and responsibility. Whenever a person is given a greater amount of responsibility than authority to do the job, the person and the organization, are likely to experience stress. Having responsibility without a balanced amount of authority is like having a job to do without the resources or tools to accomplish the job.

Stress can be particularly acute when people are naturally responsible and conscientious about their jobs. Often people deal with the stress by reverting to routine work. This damages productivity by delaying the assumption of responsibility by anyone. Unfortunately, neglecting to take responsibility results in failure, which then leads to even more stress for the organization.

A secretary I once worked with was intelligent, conscientious, and industrious. She was a model employee. One of the jobs assigned to our department was the scheduling of rooms. Since this "super" secretary had demonstrated the ability to take responsibility, she was given the task. She took immediate ownership of the job, implemented improvements, and helped to set high expectations of customer service.

This had been a challenging job in the past and had been a cause of concern. On one hand, people in the organization were not happy to see vacant rooms and facilities not being used. It became a much greater problem, however, when two groups showed up at the same time for the same room.

The job of room scheduling was being done and being done better than ever! This star employee was coming through and making the organization look professional and efficient. The customer service evaluations were excellent and the room usage was up substantially. Everyone was happy…but me.

This star employee was stressed and frustrated. She was becoming distracted at work, more irritable than before, and was even considering leaving the organization. Being a compassionate boss and not wanting to lose this valued employee, I tried to "fix" her problems. While visiting with her, I found she was spending a lot of time on room scheduling. Much more, in fact, than we had thought she would have to invest. Action was taken, some of her job duties were changed and I gave her a pep talk as well as a lot of encouragement. This solution lasted about two weeks and then we were in the same situation as before, with a frustrated employee who was about to leave.

The wrong problem was being solved. In fact, the real problem was not dealt with at all, only the symptom. Although this employee seemed overworked, the amount of work was not frustrating this employee. It was the imbalance of authority and responsibility causing stress.

This employee had been given a great amount responsibility to do the job of room scheduling. She was aware of its importance and of the past failures. By her very nature, she took ownership of the task and the responsibility. However, she was doing this job with an unequal amount of authority.

Any time she needed a room arrangement changed, refreshments made, or audio/visual equipment moved; she had to deal with two different departments without the authority to make anyone do the job in a timely manner. She was the front-line person dealing with and trying to make the customer happy, but the people who were supposed to be supporting her effort had different bosses and different levels of customer service commitment. The job of scheduling rooms was being done and being done well, but it was because of the efforts of one employee who was stressed to the verge of resigning.

The answer to the problem was simple once the dynamic of the situation was understood. There were two possible actions to reduce the stress. The amount of authority needed to be increased to match the responsibility or the amount of responsibility needed to be decreased to match the authority she was given.

Although the best solution would have been to empower her to do the work, circumstance left us only the option of reducing her responsibility. By balancing the responsibility with the authority to do the job, stress was reduced. Authority and responsibility must be balanced. When the authority given to do a job balances the responsibility given to the individual, stress is greatly reduced.

Productive—Empowered

Routine, chaos, and stress are where many organizations find themselves operating. The goal should be to reach the productive phase of authority and responsibility. In the case of the diligent employee operating with stress, the options were to reduce the responsibility or increase the authority given. Reducing the responsibility and putting the employee into a more routine work environment was the easiest solution. However, it did not make the employee or the organization more productive and reducing authority and responsibility can have the effect of squelching initiative and effort.

The difference between Productive and Routine is like the difference between addition and multiplication.

The difference between organizations working in the routine as opposed to working in the productive range is dramatic. It is like the difference between addition and multiplication. Employees working in the routine can add value to the organization, but employees who are empowered to solve their own problems and take care of customers multiply the productivity of their own work and more importantly the productivity of the group.

Getting organizations to work in the productive range, where people are empowered to do their best work requires more leadership and discipline on the part of management. In an empowered organization, the management may appear to do very little, but is in fact doing a lot for the success of the group. In routine organizations, the leadership and management direct and tell employees what to do. In this type of environment, managers are never far away and operate with the belief that if people are not directed, work will not get done. In organizations driven by routine work, this is true. Organizations depending on routine work will never be as competitive, efficient, or as powerful as organizations able to balance authority and responsibility at a high level. Organizations using low levels of authority and responsibility will predictably be filled with weak managers and leaders.

Leaders and managers developing productive groups are doing more work than their counterpart, who are content with employees operating in the routine quadrant. The work, however, is different. Leaders of productive organizations are being proactive rather than reactive. They are developing policies, procedures, processes, and setting parameters to empower people.

These leaders establish the appropriate controlling forces to direct the motivating or driving forces. Leaders of productive organizations are heavily involved in motivation and selling ideas to the workers. They want people to take ownership in their own best work.

TRANSFORMING FROM A ROUTINE
TO A PRODUCTIVE ORGANIZATION

Transforming a group from doing routine and controlled task to doing productive and empowered work will typically involve small levels of stress and possibly some chaos. The role of a leader is to monitor this stress and chaos. Having a vision of the current reality and seeing the dynamics of the situation can help a leader balance authority and responsibility to a positive outcome. Preparing people before you delegate is one of a leader's primary jobs.

Authoritarian leadership is typical in routine organizations. Leaders in these types of organizations tell people what to do, when to do it, and how it is to be done. For immature groups it may be necessary to give direct and explicit directions, but the goal of leaders should be to mature and develop the group. Authoritarian leaders are like parents of small children, constantly telling and explaining what needs to be done. They put themselves in the role of arbitrating disputes, solving problems for the followers, and taking responsibility for practically everything.

Leading a group toward a highly productive level is like parenting in many ways. The actions taken by a parent are determined by the maturity (or the ability to take responsibility) of the child. The style of leadership used in organizations also depends on the maturity and development of the group. The parent may need to use direct and explicit instruction with a small child. The young child may need to be told to do the most basic activities like brushing their teeth, putting on a jacket, or putting away their toys. As the child grows and develops, however, the parent hopes the child will become more responsible and able to do things for themselves.

Dynamic of Authority/Responsibility and Organizational Learning

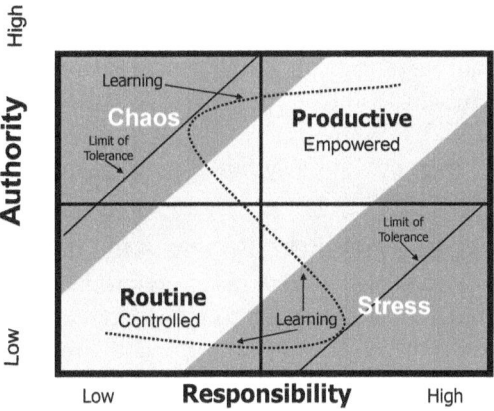

A parent is responsible for everything relating to a young child, but a parent who is doing their job will teach responsibility and will expect the child to be more accountable as they mature. It would be inappropriate to expect a small child to maintain a budget for their expenses relating to essential items like food, shelter, and clothing. As the child grows, however, they will be expected to be responsible for a small allowance, a pet, and certain household jobs. Eventually the parent will want the child to take full authority and responsibility for their life. The success of the child depends on it.

Organizations must also develop people to do their best work. New or immature employees may not be given much responsibility or authority in doing their jobs until they are developed, skilled, and able to take a higher level of authority. The goal, however, in developing a highly productive organization is to prepare people to take responsibility then empower them with authority to do their best work. Like a parent, a leader's goal is to develop people to be more self-reliant and have the ability to take high levels of authority and responsibility.

> **A leader's goal is to develop people to be more self-reliant.**

The most effective leaders are in the people development business. They take the many personalities and abilities within a group and develop individuals to perform. Preparing people before delegating authority is a sign of great leadership. Leaders should give people authority in proportion to their ability to accept responsibility. Giving people a little more authority than their current level of responsibility can extend their capacity for taking future responsibility. Although this may cause some chaos or stress in the group, leaders who understand and monitor the dynamic of authority and responsibility may find this an effective way to build responsibility.

AN EXAMPLE OF PREPARING PEOPLE FOR FUTURE SUCCESS

I learned to work in a family furniture business. Although shy at age seventeen, my father made sure I worked on the sales floor waiting on customers. At the time, I made twenty dollars plus commission on Saturdays. Considering I enjoyed free room and board, twenty dollars was good spending money.

As I began selling, I would often bring deals to my dad for his advice on how to write the ticket, arrange financing, or negotiate delivery. One Saturday, a customer I was dealing with wanted to buy a bedroom suite worth several thousand dollars. Obviously excited (about the big commission) I raced downstairs to find dad to close the deal. Dad was nowhere to be found. Returning to the customer in a cold sweat, I awkwardly hammered out the details, promised services, and made commitments I had never been empowered to make before. I breathed a big sigh of relief when the paperwork was finished and the customer's check was in the cash register.

Suddenly Dad reappeared. As I excitedly told him the details of the big sale, I quickly learned he already knew. He had been monitoring my performance the whole time. He had put me at a level of authority with which I was not accustomed or comfortable. I made some mistakes on that deal, but Dad was willing to let me learn from those mistakes. The experience increased my ability to take responsibility and prepared me to take more authority in the future.

It would have been easier for a shy kid of seventeen to work in the warehouse, and it certainly would have been easier for Dad to handle that sale, but he was developing my ability to manage and make decisions in the future. This development involved stress as I was forced to take responsibility and some chaos as I would sometimes over step the authority given me. **Developing people to take high levels of authority and responsibility is not easy,** but the long-term return on investment adds value to the group.

Building a highly productive group by balancing authority and responsibility demands leadership. This type of leadership requires the vision to analyze the abilities needed by people to do the work effectively. Leaders in these highly productive groups monitor activities, but the focus is on developing people's long-range ability to perform and solve problems instead of correcting actions for immediate results. Preparing people takes patience. It focuses on the long-term development, not just short-term solutions.

Leading highly productive groups requires the highest level of self-assurance by the leader. They must have the self-assurance to surround themselves with the best and most talented people without fearing subordinates might take over when given authority. They must be able to motivate people and create a culture while permitting innovation, creativity, and inevitably mistakes. A leader's job sometimes is to let people know the limit of tolerance for making mistakes, because they know people learn from their experience, mistakes, successes, and failures. People in the group must be willing to learn from personal failures. Leaders in these types of groups are committed to developing people. They are in the people encouragement business.

Key Points

- With Authority comes Responsibility and with Responsibility comes Authority.

- Authority without Responsibility or Responsibility without Authority is a bad situation for someone.

- Building a highly productive group requires developing people with the responsibility and competence to be given authority.

Chapter 12
Dynamic of Change:
Breaking the Force of the Status Quo for Continuous Process Improvement

> *"Man's mind, once stretched by a new idea,*
> *never regains its original dimensions."*
>
> Oliver Wendell Holmes

People fear many things: spiders, snakes, public speaking, IRS audits, vacations with the in-laws, divorce attorneys, and death. More than anything else, people fear change...even when the change is positive.

Problems and conflicts are often symptoms that positive improvements or change needs to happen in an organization. Problem solving and dealing with conflicts is typically a short-term or tactical activity for a leader, which leads to learning. Organizational learning has more of an intermediate impact and usually involves the discomfort and distress associated with conflict. Learning leads to change, which tends to have a long-term or strategic impact on the success, survival, and performance of a group.

Change is difficult to manage in groups because it involves an unseen future. Plato's *"Allegory of the Cave"* is a story about a people who have lived their whole lives chained to a wall in a cave. Their only perceptions of reality are the shadows they see on the cave wall. One day, one of them escapes to discover the world outside of the cave with fresh air, the blue sky, and the warmth of sunlight. The sunlight is at first painful, then the eyes adjust. The beautiful colors of nature are overwhelming and this person cannot wait to go back and share his discovery with the others.

Back in the cave, it is dark and the air is stale. The darkness blinds him until his eyes adjust to the environment. The others do not believe his tales of the outside world. All they see is this man blinded by the darkness. These changes and the outside world seem dangerous and may blind them—or so they reason. The people in the cave would rather live in the darkness of the cave than risk improving their lives with a positive change.

The ability to solve problems helps a group work smoothly and efficiently. Successful problem solving also builds a leader's level of trust with the group and enhances the leader's perceived competence. Technical problem solving provides a quick fix; something is wrong and action is taken to correct the situation. Some situations, however, require more than problem solving…they involved an adaptive challenge and require change.

Change is a strategic ability to have vision, influence attitudes, and direct a group through new circumstances.

Sometimes adjustments or adaptations of attitudes, values, and beliefs are required for individuals and groups to survive new challenges. Problem solving is a tactical or short-term skill in leadership. Change is a strategic ability to have vision, influence attitudes, and direct a group through new and sometimes challenging circumstances.

Conflict can indicate a need for **positive change**

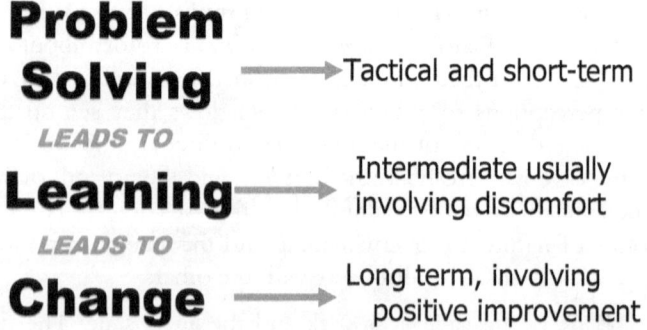

Problem Solving → Tactical and short-term

LEADS TO

Learning → Intermediate usually involving discomfort

LEADS TO

Change → Long term, involving positive improvement

Attitudes, values, and beliefs are degrees of commitment to an idea. Attitudes consist of an opinion or emotional feeling about something. Values are more pervasive than attitudes. Attitudes may fluctuate due to a variety of outside influences while values are more likely to reflect what a person really believes. Beliefs represent the deepest commitment to an ideal.

Compared to a tree, attitudes would be the leaves, values the branches, and beliefs the trunk of the tree. Accordingly, attitudes are the easiest and most apt to change like the seasonal changing of the leaves. Values are more difficult to alter but will have a bigger impact on the appearance and functioning of the tree. Changing people's beliefs, however, is complex. Like transplanting a tree, changing a person's beliefs is difficult and can only be done with great planning, care, and much effort. Knowing how to **balance the driving or motivating forces and the controlling forces is important in sustaining needed change and positive improvement.**

Perceptions and current practices are difficult to change. People cling to the status quo or the way things are, even though they may know circumstances are likely to change.

Sometimes a person can hold onto deeply held beliefs with no adverse consequences. Many times, however, the inability to adapt to new circumstance, abandon old beliefs, and change have devastating consequences. Businesses fail when they are unable to adjust to new markets and new competition. Civic groups can lose focus and become irrelevant if they fail to meet the new needs of a community. Family units and marriages can be destroyed by the inability to adapt to an ever-changing family environment. Every civilization in the history of man has had periods of decline and destruction because of their inability to adapt and change.

> *"There was a land of Cavaliers and cotton fields called the Old South. Here in this pretty world, gallantry made its last stand. Here was the last ever to be seen of knights and their ladies fair…of master and slave. Look for it only in books, for it is no more than a dream remembered, a civilization…Gone With the Wind."[12]*

These words from Margaret Mitchell's classic tale of Scarlet O'Hara and Rhett Butler tell a story of a civilization unable to

---

[12] Mitchell, Margaret, *Gone with the Wind*, The Macmillan Company, 1936

adapt to new circumstances, new challenges, new attitudes, and a nation's evolving moral conscience. Many groups are ready to "fight the Yankees" when the real battle is preparing the group to adapt to a new reality. Shaping the group's values, beliefs, and actions to meet the needs of a changing environment is real work for leadership.

Failure to adapt to new circumstances by holding on to the "way things are" puts any group at risk of extinction. Creating positive improvement, changing, and adjusting to meet the reality of the future is the responsibility and challenge of leadership.

We live in a time, which may well be defined as the age of change. Technological, social, and occupational transitions occur at a lightening pace. Parents who worked in careers for thirty and forty years see their adult children changing careers multiple times in today's work environment. Change today is inevitable. Whether the change is positive or negative to an individual is optional, depending on the individual's attitude, ability, and aptitude to change.

Force of the Status Quo

The force of status quo and the resistance to change is a common problem for organizations and it can be a dangerous force. People have to adapt and change to meet the challenges of the future. Intelligence and strength are no longer the main ingredients to survival and success. The ability to see the need for change, adapt to a new environment, and create a preferred future now becomes the essential elements to survival.

The horse once dominated personal transportation. The horse required whole industries to support this mode of transportation. Nearly every town had a blacksmith, a livery stable, a leather shop, feed store, and people to shovel the streets to support this form of transportation. Those jobs and supporting industry do not exist anymore because the market changed. There is still a smaller industry of specialists servicing the horse industry, but it is not the major part of the economy it once was. The desires of customers and the technology of transportation outdated the horse and buggy, replacing it with the automobile.

Think of how many businesses in every community serve the automobile industry today. Gas stations, car dealerships, auto parts stores, and insurance agencies all service the new transportation.

People who were unwilling to change from the horse and buggy economy to meet new demands, refine their skills, or find new markets, were out of work and out of business.

Imagine if a new technology were to emerge tomorrow, which was cheaper, faster, and more convenient than the automobile (it will happen someday.) The effects would be gigantic. New businesses would appear and old ones would disappear. The transformation would be inevitable, but inevitably, some people would resist. They would hang on to the established or known, even though the new and improved was coming.

It might sound far-fetched to think of a new technology replacing the automobile. However, vacuum tube manufacturers, typewriter companies, mimeograph machines, eight-track cassette players, vinyl records, as well as many other items, which used to be state of the art, have met the same force of change. Nostalgia is happening today, we just don't know it yet.

Market forces are powerful and they will overwhelm the force of the status quo. One of my best friends inherited a television sales and repair

Nostalgia is happening today, we just don't know it yet.

business from his father, which he ran for several years. It was a good business that was well run and profitable. The force of change, however, challenged the status quo. Televisions had been expensive and customers were willing to pay to get them fixed. However, televisions became cheaper, so cheap in fact people quit having them fixed. The manufacturing technology was so good, television sets were not only cheaper they were better with more features and superior pictures.

What had been an investment in the home quickly transformed into a disposable item people used and threw away. This friend had to change, to evolve with the market forces. Television repair was no longer practical. If he had tried to resist the market forces and stay with the status quo (natural human behavior), he would have been forced out of business. Instead, he changed. First, he repaired VCRs, then computers, and then used his expertise to get into technical training. By adapting with the market forces and abandoning the status quo, he was able to direct and influence the preferred future instead of being swept away by the inevitable.

Years ago, I went on a float trip on the Illinois River in eastern Oklahoma. The Illinois River is a beautiful, gentle river, which provides as oasis from the summer heat. There are few rapids and the flow of water is steady and relaxing. This day, after getting out of the canoe, I was enjoying floating on my back down the river. The flow of the water seemed tame. Since I was moving with the current of the river, I was unaware of its force. I could not even feel the current moving me until my leg became caught under a log submerged under the water.

The force of change is unrelenting. It is better to understand and work with the forces of change then to be overwhelmed by them.

Suddenly the force of status quo held me in place and the gentle force of the flowing river was much greater than expected or realized. The water was pushing me further under the snag and I found myself caught between two opposing forces.

Fortunately, there were other people there to help me out of my predicament, but the lesson of being stuck in the status quo was long remembered. It is more constructive to work with the existing forces than to work against them.

Dynamic of Status Quo and Change

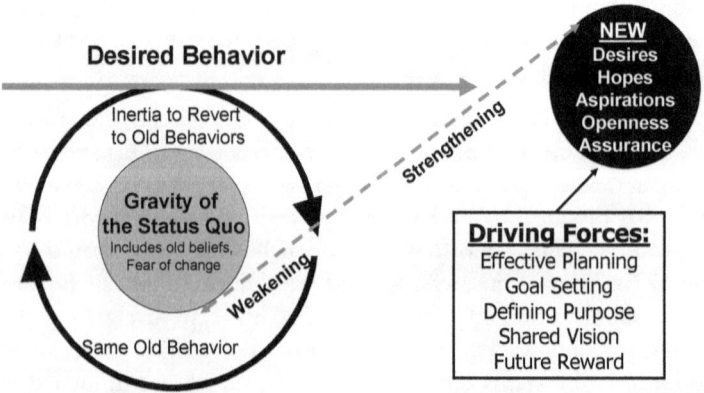

The force of the water in the river is much like the force of change compared to the stagnant force of the status quo. The river can be successfully navigated, if you look ahead and work with the flow of the water. When you are caught in the snag of the status quo, the driving force of change will pull you down.

The gravity of the status quo includes old beliefs and a fear of change. From early childhood, unlearned fears are caused by unexpected or strange situations. Although many fears are rational and provide safety, this fear of the unknown seems to stay with most people for all of their life. **Fear** is one of the strongest forces affecting the behavior of individuals. Although people sometimes like to fantasize about adventure and the unknown, in real life we cling to the status quo. Fear is a negative motivator because it only moves people to avoid something. It is also a barrier to vision, destroys positive attitude, and retards self-assurance.

Over time, fear can cause people to be influenced by another factor, habit. **Habit** becomes another strong force determining how people will react in situations. The inertia of habits moves people back to old behaviors and keeps them in familiar environments, which they perceive as safe. Habits develop over time and often habits develop for no constructive purpose.

New and stronger desires must overcome the old fears and habits for change to happen. The change must happen with preparation and within a person's limit of self-assurance. When someone becomes unsure, they revert to old fears and habits…the force of the status quo. If fear and habit are the negative side of motivation, then hope and aspiration would be the positive aspect of motivation. The dynamic of **planning (See Chapter 8, Dynamic of Planning)** can be a powerful tool to identify and focus attention on new, preferable goals, desires, objectives, hopes, and aspirations.

Continuous process improvement is something many business organizations attempt to implement to stay competitive and viable in today's business environment. This philosophy looks at a business operation in terms of value added activities compared to non-value added activities. It seems simple; spend more resources on value added activities (things the customer is willing to pay for) while streamlining or eliminating non-value added activities (things the customer does not particularly care to pay for).

Business organizations develop many activities over time, which have archaic or no purpose at all. Processes are in place because they have "always been done that way." There are several causes for inefficient business practices, but one of the biggest factors is fear and habit. For example, a supervisor is promoted into a job they are not completely comfortable with. The fear of someone finding out they do not know everything keeps the supervisor from asking that important question, "Why?" Instead of looking at processes and their real purpose, the tendency is to copy, emulate, and do things the way the previous supervisor did. Chances are the former supervisor did the same thing and after time, the web of the status quo mires the business in inefficiency.

An incredible amount of human behavior is done each day by habit. Habits control people perhaps more than by any other force. These habits are forged over time, sometimes consciously, but usually sub-consciously. Habits can lead to productive practices but they become a hindrance to being open-minded, creative, and adaptable to meet the changing needs of today and tomorrow. To succeed and survive, people must be able to perceive the challenges of the future and break the force of the status quo to meet those challenges. To break the force of status quo a person must develop a high level of self-assurance and be able to see things for what they are. Creating and controlling new desires can help a person break free from the status quo and the fear of change.

The Nature of Learning

Learning is a permanent change in behavior, which comes from knowledge, practice, or experience. Human beings are learning from birth until the day they die. Learning pervades everything a person does and thinks. It plays a role in the language people speak, the customs people have, the attitudes, the beliefs, and the perception a person has about life. Learning is an essential element in a person's ability to adapt, survive, and succeed. Learning also plays a role in maladaptive and destructive character traits, which become a barrier to a person's success.

Learning often involves pain or negative consequences to actions. Aristotle once said, "We cannot learn without pain." He also said, "What we have to learn, we learn by doing." Aristotle's insights into how humans learn are as true today as they were in ancient times. Think of how a baby learns to walk...by trial and error. Falling down is a somewhat painful experience so the child adjusts their technique in attempting to walk to lessen the pain. The child will also attempt to repeat actions, which bring a measure of success in the trial-and-error process.

Avoidance to pain is a strong motivator in learning. Most natural learning occurs when pain is involved. Most basic behaviors are learned by avoidance. The stove is hot. It hurts to touch. Do not touch it any more. Stick your tongue to an ice tray just once...it freezes, it hurts, do not do that anymore. An electrical outlet has a charge that will shock you. Get shocked just once and the tendency is to have more respect for the nature of electricity.

Change and breaking the force of the status quo requires learning. Sometimes short-term pain, discomfort, and disequilibria of problems and conflict are involved in this learning process. The pain associated with a group may not be physical pain, but the anxiety and distress of changing attitudes, values, and beliefs can be just as acute as physical pain.

Physical pain can be an indicator or symptom of more serious health concerns. Ignoring the pain or treating the pain instead of the problem can have serious consequences. Likewise, disequilibrium in groups is often an indicator of more serious organizational problems. Dealing with superficial issues and the discomfort of a situation, while ignoring the root causes of problems, can have serious consequences. Leaders are responsible for creating the vision to see the real challenges of the situation and to guide the group through adaptive changes to meet the environment.

The status quo is a powerful force and people may not be willing to make positive and necessary changes until pain and discomfort force a change. In groups, there are sometimes gaps causing the feeling of distress and anxiety. Gaps between existing values and needed values, between values and behaviors, between market needs and current ability, and between future opportunities and current capacity are examples of motivating forces for change.

Leadership's Role

People often think the role of leader is one of setting the direction, giving the marching orders, motivating the followers, and solving the problems of the group. These traits may be useful in some leadership situations, but often the challenge of leadership requires more. Sometimes leaders must prepare the group to face problems, new challenges, and make changes to deal with the new situation.

A leader may have the difficult task of breaking the status quo and leading the group through the adaptive process of change. There may be gaps between existing values and needed values, between stated values and real values, between current capacity and the needs of the marketplace or future opportunities.

The hard work of leadership includes identifying these gaps and the barriers to success involving change while preparing the group to make the required adaptations. Learning and change often come with some pain and discomfort. Leadership involves controlling the learning process in doses the group can handle. If the group does not feel safe in the change process, they are likely to replace the current leader with one that makes them feel safer. This is rarely constructive for the group, because holding on to old and false values and beliefs will eventually force a change, which may not be as constructive.

For leaders to implement changes, they must break the force of the status quo by overcoming the fear and habits of the group. **A leader can focus attention on new desires and new goals for the group by effectively using group planning.** The rewards and benefits of the new desires must be more important than the fear of change causing people to revert to old habits. To lead people through change, the leader will need to build up the assurance in the group. Open feedback and reinforcement will help nurture the group's assurance level. Permission will need to be given to make mistakes. The breaking of old habits may need to occur in stages and new habits may need to be developed as substitutes for old behaviors. The leader will need to monitor the process to make sure the work of change does not outstrip the group's level of assurance and ability to adapt to new behaviors.

Leaders are often forced to be the truth bearers and the change agents for a group. This is a difficult task at best and can be perilous for the leader. Understanding the dynamics in a situation—the driving forces and controlling forces—to predict how people in the group will act and react is needed by a leader to do the difficult work of preparing a group for strategic change.

Key Points

- Change is inevitable, but the misery is optional.

- Problems and conflicts are often symptoms that positive change and organizational learning needs to occur.

- Identifying the new environment and preparing people for constructive change is one of the responsibilities of leadership.

- Breaking the force of the status quo requires overcoming fear and habit while identifying new goals and desires by using effective group planning.

PART IV

Dealing with Difficult People

Effectively dealing with other people is an important leadership ability. Recognizing the driving forces and controlling forces causing people to act and react as they do can help a leader motivate and influence a group toward greater success. Identifying destructive attitudes and dealing with their impact on a group can bring harmony, peace, and productivity to an organization.

Chapter 13
Dynamic of Character:
Assurance, Attitude, and Actions

> *"Character is like a tree and reputation like its shadow.*
> *The shadow is what we think of it; the tree is the real thing."*
>
> Abraham Lincoln

Water, the most abundant resource on Earth, contains the basic elements of hydrogen and oxygen, more specifically two atoms of hydrogen and one atom of oxygen. This is basic physics; physical things are made up of more fundamental material called elements. Character is similar in construction because it also has basic, fundamental elements. Knowing these elements of character helps in understanding other people and their actions. Recognizing the potential influence and driving forces involved in these elements of character can even help in understanding ourselves.

What are these elements of character, the stuff of which character and integrity are made? A host of descriptive words and ideas describe character traits but all fit into three basic elements. The self-***assurance*** one possesses, the ***attitude*** with which they see the world, and the ***actions*** they take. Assurance, attitude, and actions bind together to determine the integrity and very essence of a person's character.

Character is the combination of qualities distinguishing the moral and ethical traits of an individual. It is a blend of a person's self-assurance, attitude, and actions, which classify the quality of their behavior. Character is different from personality, because character is a qualitative definition of what a person thinks, believes, and does. Character involves integrity. It is what a person will do when no one is watching. Doing the right thing is not always easy but it is always the right thing to do. People of integrity possess the elements of character necessary to do the right thing. Abraham Lincoln once said, "Character is like a tree and reputation like its shadow. The shadow is what we think of it the tree is the real thing."

Elements of Character

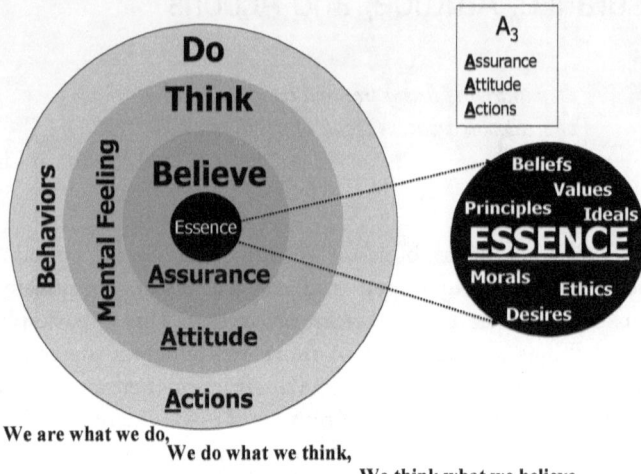

We are what we do,
We do what we think,
We think what we believe

The three elements of character are interrelated in determining how a person acts, thinks, and believes. Deep inside the assurance element is the essence or spiritual center of person including their beliefs, values, principles, ideals, morals, ethics, and desires. Surrounding a person's essence is the element of assurance. Assurance is close to the core value of what a person really believes about themselves and others. Attitudes are more observable and involve the mental feelings a person has about their environment. Unlike assurance and attitude, actions are very observable. Actions are what people do. They are the specific behaviors and choices dictating the success or failure of an individual.

ASSURANCE

The level of assurance a person has in himself or herself is essential to quality character development. It is how people view themselves. Assurance is invisible and often a mystery to others. It is difficult to influence someone else's assurance, but self-assurance has a long-term effect on the success and character of the individual. A common mistake leaders make in dealing with other people is to have an expectation of affecting this element of a person's character. Positively affecting a person's self-esteem is a difficult and time-consuming task. Unfortunately, the ability to tear down and negatively influence another person's self-esteem is more easily done.

Optimistic attitudes and success fuel positive self-assurance. The benefits of positive self-assurance include empathy toward others, innovation, self-reliance, and humility. Some of the consequences of having low self-assurance include cynical attitudes, dependence on others for happiness, an arrogant demeanor, and bad habits. Positive attitude and success are builders of assurance while fear, failure, and negative attitudes are the great destroyers of self-assurance.

> **Optimistic attitudes and success fuel positive self-assurance.**

ATTITUDE

Attitude is a mental feeling. It is how a person views the world. **(See Chapter 14, Dynamic of Attitude)** The element of attitude is slightly visible to other people and can be somewhat affected by personalities and situations within a group. Assurance is what a person really is while attitude is how a person feels about things. Positively affecting a person's assurance is almost impossible. Positively influencing a person's attitude is more possible yet still difficult.

Assurance and attitude will have a great influence on how a person acts and behaves. The American philosopher and psychologist William James wrote, "Human beings, by changing the inner attitude of their minds, can change the outer aspects of their lives."

ACTIONS

Actions and behaviors are a reflection and demonstration of a person's assurance and attitude. Assurance is almost invisible, attitude is more translucent, but actions are very visible. Since actions can be observed and documented, they can also be affected and manipulated. Driving forces and controlling forces can influence a person's behavior and actions. Documenting behaviors and making people responsible is an effective method in influencing a person's attitude and building their self-assurance. Consequences and rewards can also be used to alter the habits and behaviors of an individual. Actions are the element of character where learning happens.

Actions are the outward product of what a person thinks, feels and believes.

Actions are the outward product of what a person thinks, feels, and believes. As fruit identifies the type and quality of a tree, the quality of person is identified by the quality of their actions. Actions are the product of a person's assurance and attitude. We are what we do (Actions), we do what we think (Attitude), and we think what we believe (Assurance). The quality of a person's actions determine the quality of a person's success, failure, and character.

In dealing with difficult people, it is important to remember that choices directly affect **Actions** and **Attitude**. **Actions** and **Attitude** indirectly affect **Assurance**. To effectively deal with destructive people, a leader must deal with the person's **Actions**

In dealing with difficult people, it is important to remember that choices directly affect actions and attitude.

and behaviors. **Actions** can be affected by using driving force (motivation), controlling force (monitoring), making the person responsible for actions, documentation, learning (consequences and rewards), and by modeling. **Effectively dealing with difficult people requires dealing with their actions and behaviors** before attempting to change their assurance or attitude.

DYNAMIC OF CHARACTER MODEL ARCHETYPES

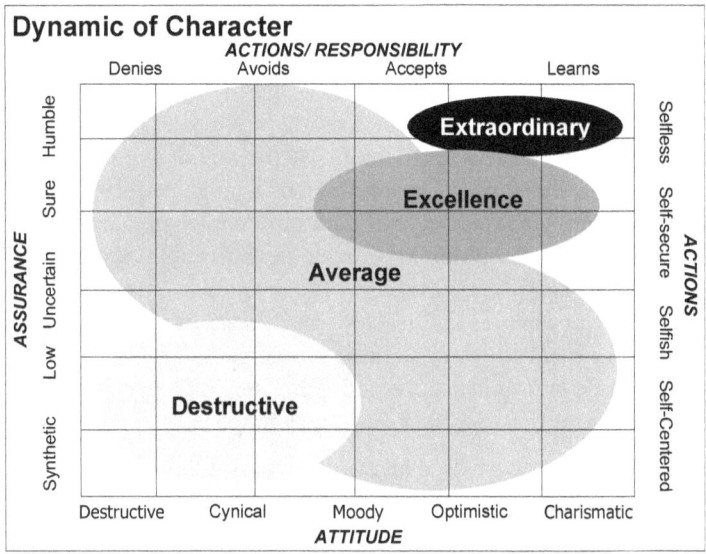

Leaders are required to motivate, understand, and work with people, who often have widely varied backgrounds, values, personalities, and character. The **Dynamic of Character** model is a tool to help define character archetypes from extraordinary to destructive based on subjective observations of assurance, attitude, and actions. The model defines four character archetypes, **destructive**, **average**, **excellent**, and **extraordinary**. An archetype is a pattern or example of typical characteristics or behavior. This model is a hypothesis of how the elements of character affect a person's behavior in a group.

The three elements of character: assurance, attitude, and actions, are represented in varying degrees on the model. The level of assurance is measured from synthetic (or pretended assurance), to low assurance, to uncertain assurance, to being sure in oneself to the highest level of assurance, the ability to be humble and put the needs of others first. The levels of attitude range from the most negative (the destructive level), to cynical, moody, optimistic and finally to the highest attitude level, the charismatic attitude (who is the person able to create positive attitudes in others.) **(See Chapter 14, Dynamic of Attitude)**

Actions are measured in two ways, by relationship to others and by responsibility. Relation to others moves from being self-centered, to selfish, self-secured, to the highest level selflessness. The level of responsibility goes from the tendency to deny responsibility, to avoiding responsibility, to accepting responsibility, to the highest level, learning from mistakes and taking responsibility.

Measuring the elements, particularly assurance and attitude, is not meant to be precise evaluations of the qualitative character of an individual. The model is not intended to judge people and assign them a static position on the model. People are continuously vacillating from one point to another in the model depending on the situation and their elements of character in response to the situation. For example, a person may feel assured and confident with family members and familiar situations. This same person may be uncertain and unsure about himself or herself in various social situations in which they are not as familiar.

The highest level, the extraordinary, is that one-in-a-million person functioning at the highest levels of assurance, attitude, and actions. The extraordinary character type represents the ideal person for working in a group. Even the most outstanding people only occasionally demonstrate extraordinary characteristics.

A leader can also use this model to examine their character type in seeking to continually improve leadership potential for creating vision and building influence. Striving for the level of assurance, attitude, and actions needed for the extraordinary character type will result in leadership that is more effective.

Extraordinary Character Archetypes

The extraordinary character archetype will be that rare person having the ultimate traits fostering success. This character type has tremendous self-confidence, which provides them with a good, positive self-image. Their confidence and assurance in themselves permit them to be innovative, enthusiastic about life, caring about other people, and positive. The attitude of extraordinary people, not only is positive, but also creates positive energy and attitudes in others.

The extraordinary person is fearless. They are visionary, goal oriented, and super achievers. They are permission givers, seeing innovative alternatives, which they are not afraid to choose. The extraordinary do not fear mistakes but look at them as opportunities to learn. Learning is a philosophy they use in life.

They learn from mistakes, from triumphs, from failure, and most of all from life. The extraordinary person will seek out problems because they know problems and challenges present opportunity. Their confidence allows them to forgive themselves for mistakes, to learn, and start over.

The extraordinary person does not wage war on life without a plan. The planning process is ingrained in everything they do. Positive self-image allows them to understand themselves, their strengths, and their weaknesses. They have a good vision of where they want to go and the discipline to achieve their goals.

In Abraham Maslow's research on the motivation of people through the hierarchy of needs, he searched out people functioning at the highest levels of personal success to study. These subjects he described as self-actualized. Maslow concluded there were no "perfect" self-actualized people but only people coming close to reaching these levels. Maturity and life experiences were more important than education level or environment according to Maslow. He wrote, "I had to conclude that self-actualization of the sort I had found in my older subjects was not possible in our society for young, developing people."[13] Reaching the highest levels of self-actualization or extraordinary character traits takes time, development, and maturity.

Extraordinary character people demonstrate a variety of characteristics, beginning with a more efficient perception of reality...the ability to create a clear vision of the current situation. These people have the ability to not only see things the way they are, but are also more comfortable with this truth. They are more accepting of self, others, nature, and their environment. Extraordinary people also tend to be spontaneous, simple, and natural. They have a marked lack of artificiality.

> **Extraordinary people have the ability to not only see things the way they are, but are also more comfortable with this truth.**

---

[13] Maslow, Abraham H., *Motivation and Personality*, 2nd Edition, Harper and Row, 1970

These people are problem centered instead of ego centered, able to focus on events outside of themselves. Extraordinary people are autonomous, self-reliant, and independent. They are able to work well with other people and environments, while displaying the highest levels of self-assurance.

Working with and understanding Extraordinary people

Seek and value their counsel and advice. Be observant when working with and for this person because you will learn a great deal. Do what you say you will do when dealing with them, never make excuses, and admit when you make a mistake. Do not be offended when they say no. Extraordinary people are supremely self-assured and will be honest with you, because they do not need your approval. They will be polite, generous, and humble. Listen intently to what they say while being professional, specific and prepared.

Excellent Character Archetypes

The excellent character archetypes are achievement oriented. They are interested and curious about a variety of things with a strong desire to succeed. The excellent character type people are able to really get things done. Many times, they will implement the innovative ideas of the extraordinary.

Excellent character archetypes have many of the traits of the extraordinary person but usually not to the same degree. They are self-assured and have a good self-image, but are not as totally confident in themselves and the direction their life is going as the extraordinary character type. They have a positive attitude, but their positive feelings come from achievements rather than the absolute assurance they have in themselves. The excellent person generally tries to prove themselves and their worth more than the extraordinary person does.

Achieving goals is very much a part of the excellent character type. However, they are usually not as fluent in the planning process or at visioning as the extraordinary person. Although they have a general idea about the goals they want to obtain, they are not as specific about those goals or the actions required to achieve them.

The excellent character archetype is very similar to the extraordinary character archetype. What distinguishes the extraordinary character archetype is their supreme self-assurance. The extraordinary character archetype has little need for approval by others, is insensitive to criticism, has heighten abilities to learn from mistakes, can easily give approval and credit to others, and has a humble demeanor.

Working with and understanding Excellent people

This type of person will get things done and be valuable to any group. Feel comfortable sharing your goals and dreams with them. Listen for their input and suggestions because they will be valuable. Give constructive feedback because these people take criticism well and are always looking to improve. They will take calculated risks when they believe they can win. Challenge these people and communicate in terms of benefits and values when asking for their help. Count on these people to follow through when they give you their word because they will rarely let you down.

Average Character Archetypes

Most people encountered in life are the average character archetype. They do not have the self-confidence and self-assurance to operate at the same levels personally and interpersonally as the excellent character archetype. They have been conditioned to be average by the messages they have received all of their life like; "don't talk to strangers," "don't make waves," "be careful" and "don't make mistakes."

Many times, leaders themselves have the traits of the average character archetype. The skill-set that gets people to the top of the organizational chart are not always the same characteristics needed to lead. True leadership requires influence and vision. Having the positional title of leader does not always equate to having the necessary skills to lead.

> The skill-set that gets people to the top of the organizational chart are not always the same characterized needed to lead.

Average people worry about what others think of them. They constantly seek approval from others because they do not really believe they are important. Their attitudes are moody. When things occasionally go well, they can appear positive but when things go bad, (and they always do sometime) they become negative. They take little responsibility or authority for their life. They prefer to float through life accepting what happens to them while taking little action to change their long-term destination.

Average people are motivated by survival. They want to make it through the day, week, month, or year, to "survive" until the end of the day, the weekend, vacation, or retirement. They are not "today" people but "someday" people, waiting for their ship to come in constantly thinking, "if only this would happen or that would happen my life would get better." The average person thinks they think but are in reality fence sitters and polltakers waiting to follow someone else's lead. They like to play it safe, avoid mistakes, cause no problems, and make it through. The extraordinary plan to win, the excellent win through effort, and the average hopes to win.

Working with and understanding Average people

Do not have high expectations of this person. They are satisfied with "getting along." Remember not to exclude them because they have little self-confidence and need to feel like they belong. They like you to make decisions and be responsible. They are task oriented so give clear instructions and tell them exactly what to do. Be empathetic and listen to them but be careful not to let them have all your time because they will take all that you will give them. Make them feel important and worthwhile because they need to believe in themselves. Display extraordinary and excellent leadership characteristics to these people and they will follow you because they like to be around a winner.

Average character archetypes generally have restricted ability to adapt to new challenges. Their lack of self-assurance causes them to cling to the status quo. In crises or times of extreme change, a leader will need to be direct and explicit in their instructions to the average character type.

Destructive Character Archetypes

The destructive character archetype has little real self-esteem. Often they have a synthetic or false self-image, pretending to be confident, knowledgeable, and even arrogant. They deal with lack of self-esteem by being critical of others around them. Since they do not believe they can achieve, they try to tear down and put down other people to make themselves feel better. They do not understand people and suspect others are out to get them. Although this type of person has poor self-image, they will often compensate by putting on a veneer of arrogance and conceit. Destructive character archetypes are self-absorbed and self-centered to the point of believing everyone and everything revolves around them.

The destructive character person has a negative attitude about nearly everything. They will always have a long list of people and things they do not like. In their minds, almost everyone is incompetent, untrustworthy, and wrong—except them. They are often so self-centered they believe most people are working and plotting against them.

These people believe the world owes them something. They are the takers and users in life. Their goal is to get something for nothing and give nothing of themselves to anyone at any time.

Destructive character archetypes believe the world owes them something.

Destructive character archetypes cause problems everywhere. They want authority to have the world the way they want it but do not want responsibility for anything including their own actions. Their low levels of self-assurance will not allow them to admit mistakes. Destructive character people will always blame someone else for their mistakes. They are not only destructive to groups but their lack of self-assurance, a proper attitude, or positive actions usually doom them to personal failure also.

Working with and understanding Destructive people

Realize this type of person takes a great deal of time, energy, and emotion. They will shoot down ideas and give reasons why you will not be able to achieve success. Destructive people are experts at losing and try to bring others to their level. Be mentally strong around this person and be careful about your attitude because their goal is to make others unhappy. Make sure any and all agreements are clearly understood and if possible in writing. Although it is generally a good idea to not burn bridges and keep relationships, you should make every effort to terminate these relationships and avoid this type to person when possible.

ATTRIBUTES OF CHARACTER ARCHETYPES

	Extraordinary	Excellent	Average	Destructive
Relation to others	Self-less	Self-Secure	Selfish	Self-Centered
Assurance	Totally Assured	Assured	Unsure	Synthetic Confidence
Attitude	Creates Positive Attitudes in Others	Optimistic	Moody	Cynical or Destructive
View of the Future	Visionary	Goal Oriented	Task Oriented	Disoriented
Objectivity	Third Person	Objective	Short Sighted	Prejudiced
Mistakes	Learns from Mistakes	Accepts Mistakes	Avoids Mistakes	Denies Mistakes
Motivation	Actualize (Living)	Success	Survival	Denial
Thinking Ability	Are Dreamers	Are Thinkers	Think they Think	Don't Think
Achievements	Permission Givers	Follow the Extraordinary	Poll Takers	Say It Can't Be Done
Problem Solving	Seek Problems	Solve Problems	Avoid Problems	Cause Problems

LEADERSHIP'S ROLE

The three elements of character; **assurance**, **attitude**, and **actions** combine to determine the quality and integrity of a person's character. Unlike personality, character has a qualitative nature defined by the experiences, discipline, and environment of the individual. Character archetypes are classified as **destructive**, **average**, **excellent**, or **extraordinary** depending on how a person has developed their elements of character.

People are always changing and developing. One of leadership's greatest challenges is to prepare and develop people. By understanding how people's actions are often determined by their self-assurance and attitude, it becomes incumbent on the leader to attempt to build a person's self-assurance and positively influence their attitude by effectively dealing with their actions and behaviors. Leaders understanding the **Dynamic of Character** are better equipped to develop the talents of the people they lead. Exceptional leaders develop the people they lead to be new and better leaders themselves.

The **Dynamic of Character** model helps leaders understand others better and allows a leader to work more effectively with different types of people. The **Dynamic of Character** model is also a tool to help evaluate where the leader is in character development and where they need to improve. Developing the highest levels of assurance, having the most positive attitude, and demonstrating responsible actions help in achieving extraordinary levels of leadership.

A common mistake for leaders is attempting to psycho-analyze and fix people, particularly the average and destructive character archetypes. Well-intentioned leaders desiring to develop people in the group will attempt to improve the assurance and attitude of a person (which has taken a lifetime to develop) in a short amount of time. Significantly influencing the assurance and attitude of another person is difficult to impossible.

When trying to effectively influence a person's performance and character a leader must deal with the actions and behaviors. Actions directly affect a person's attitude. Actions and attitude in combination can in the long-term affect a person's assurance. Actions and behaviors can be influenced by using driving forces (motivation), controlling forces (monitoring), making the person responsible for actions by documenting behaviors, teaching the consequences and rewards of behaviors, and by positive modeling from the leader.

In dealing with destructive people, try to document actions, focus on behaviors not personalities, be explicit in your expectations, and put important desired behaviors in writing to avoid misunderstandings. Work on actions and behaviors before attempting to change attitudes and self-esteem. Constantly reinforce positive and negative behaviors. Do not let destructive people drag you to their level or overreact. Be proactive in dealing with behaviors instead of reactive.

It will always be easier to adjust your attitude and actions than it will be to affect another person's mindset. Modeling the highest levels of maturity, self-assurance, positive attitude, constructive decisions, and behaviors is doable and will have long-term, positive influence on the people around you.

Key Points

- A person's **Assurance**, **Attitude**, and **Actions** defines their character.
- Effective leaders are able to analyzes and examine, in a non-judgmental and objective way, the character of others.
- To most effectively deal with other people, particularly the Destructive Character Types, focus on behaviors and actions to help influence attitude and assurance.
- Leaders should strive to model high levels of assurance, attitude, and actions to maximize their leadership potential.

Chapter 14
Dynamic of Attitude:
Strategies for Dealing with Difficult People

"Nothing can stop the man with the right mental attitude from achieving his goal; nothing on earth can help the man with the wrong mental attitude."
Thomas Jefferson

Attitude is a volatile element of character affecting individual behavior and group morale. Learning to identify, understand, and work with people having different attitude archetypes increases harmony and effectiveness in a group. Developing a constructive personal attitude is important, but dealing with the attitudes of others is equally important. Recognizing destructive attitudes and implementing strategies to neutralize their detrimental effects can mean the difference between success and bedlam in an organization.

Attitudes are how people view, interpret, and believe what they perceive as reality. These learned responses are taught by the environment and experiences occurring at formative times in a person's development. Parental influences, peer interactions, education, and other factors affect a person's attitude over time. Attitudes are shrouded in invisibility and are only observed by the way people act and react to situations.

A good attitude involves a conscience choice and the discipline to prepare for a positive mindset.

Although attitudes are learned, people have the power and responsibility to choose their attitude. To choose one's attitude in any given circumstance is to choose one's own destiny—to empower one's own self. People can change their outlook after realizing what their attitude is and how their mindset affects their life. Happiness requires contentment and contentment happens through attitude. Developing a more constructive attitude involves creating a vision for the present and knowing how to influence a more positive future. A good attitude involves a conscience choice and the discipline to prepare for a positive mindset.

Specific versus General Attitudes

Like fingerprints, attitudes vary and are distinctive to an individual. Attitudes can be specific reactions to certain stimulus or general feelings a person has about the environment surrounding them. **Specific attitudes** will vary widely depending on the stimulus causing the attitude. **General attitudes**, however, are more pervasive and likely formed over time by a variety of life-experience factors. Individuals' general attitudes often affect morale and performance of a group more acutely. General attitudes are characterized by consistency and pervasiveness among individuals in a group.

There is a tendency to classify people as either positive or negative personalities when discussing attitude. Positive attitude people are usually categorized as being good and negative attitude people as being bad. This simplistic outlook does little to help understand how attitudes affect organizations and how this dynamic can be managed. Positive and negative are also qualitative measures not entirely appropriate to describe learned responses.

Specific attitudes are mental feelings or opinions about certain circumstances or situations. People may have a predominate attitude but these mental feelings are constantly changing and vacillating. There are extremes to these mental feelings, and people are always in between these extremes. Positive attitude extremes include learning, thankfulness, optimism, happiness, contentment, enthusiasm, assurance, and peace of mind. Negative attitude extremes include competing, resentfulness, cynicism, sadness, anxiety, apathy, worry, and guilt. Few people are totally positive or negative. The goal is to influence people toward choosing a more positive mental feeling.

Selfishness is a major barrier to building harmony in a group. Attitude extremes are related to selflessness versus selfishness. Selfless people will tend to have a mental feeling toward other people of respect, humility, love, kindness, forgiving, giving, joyfulness, patience, and encouragement. Self-centered attitudes will tend to be rude, arrogant, hateful, spiteful, vengeful, taking, jealous, angry, and critical.

Negative attitudes may be a barrier to a person's success but they are not always indicative of a person's character. The self-assurance, and particularly the actions, of a person (not their predisposed attitude toward an action) are equally important. The general attitude or outlook of a person has a tremendous effect on groups. Understanding the Dynamic of Attitude can help explain how groups act and react.

Characteristics of Moody Attitude People

Most people are not dogmatically "negative or positive" attitude people...they have moody attitudes. Their specific attitude or outlook is subject to change depending on the situation. A person wakes up in the morning and finds the weather is beautiful. It's Friday, it's payday, and wonderful weekend looms. The person is likely to have a positive attitude or outlook that day meaning they are happy, agreeable, and perhaps even pleasant to be around.

The same person wakes up to find it is cold and rainy with several unpleasant tasks to do at work. The milk is gone for breakfast and his or her favorite sweater has shrunk. It is not going to take much more for this person to have a sour, unhappy, and unpleasant disposition or attitude. Most of us are subject to shifts in our attitude based on the surroundings we face on a specific day. Moody attitude people are always changing their disposition and in groups, there is a contest to affect their attitude.

> Moody attitude people are reactive. They let outside forces dictate their state of mind. They don't take responsibility for their attitudes and are too quick to blame others.

Moody attitude people are vulnerable to the culture and groupthink of their surroundings. They go with the flow, letting other people and outside circumstance determine the way they feel. They follow the herd. Their beliefs and attitudes will often be a barometer for the overall morale of the group.

Dynamic of Attitude

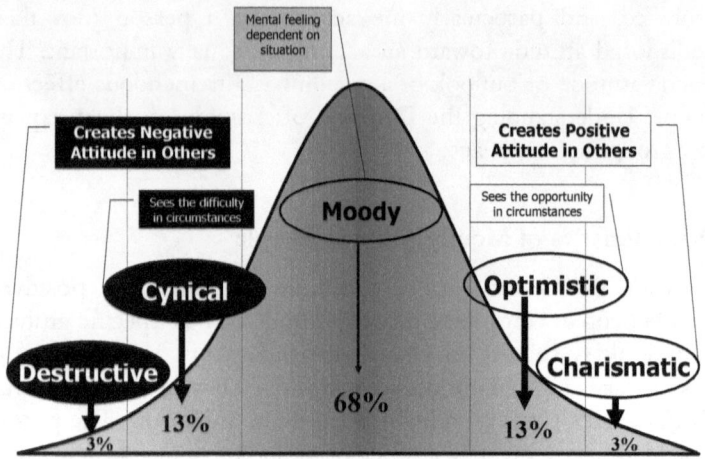

Moody attitude people must be led or their disposition becomes more negative. Organizations with poor morale usually have many moody attitude people who are not being directed and led to a more positive outlook. Without leadership, direction, and motivation moody attitude people tend to let their attitude drift to the lowest common denominator. Groupthink is a powerful force in organizations and it is caused by the effect moody attitude people let others have on them. **(See Chapter 5, Dynamic of Groupthink)**

Characteristics of Optimistic Attitude People

Some people are positive or optimistic, regardless of outside stimuli happening around them. Optimistic people have a great reputation because they are pleasant and agreeable to be around. They are "can do" people who will generally get the job done. Optimists are less common than moody personalities and even the most positive person will have a bad day. Optimists have a naturally positive outlook about life but even people who are not naturally optimistic can train themselves to be more positive.

Optimists have high energy and enthusiasm. They are apt to be goal and achievement oriented. Optimistic attitudes can be strong driving forces in a group. The positive attitude person is pleasant to be around and will be open to new ideas. They take constructive criticism well and look to improve. Positive attitude people believe the best about people and sometimes are naïve to the character and motives of others, particularly destructive people. Optimists are idealist and like to believe the best about everyone and every situation.

Becoming more optimistic requires a high degree of self-assurance and the ability to focus on the values, ideals, and beliefs important to that person. Optimistic people are likely to be good planners and goal setters who are able to focus their energies. They have learned to respect people. True optimists genuinely like other people and want them to succeed.

> **Becoming more optimistic requires a high degree of self-assurance.**

Characteristics of Cynical People

A predisposition to be negative and faultfinding about practically everything is a characteristic of cynical attitude people. Although these people are usually categorized as being negative attitudes, cynical is a better description because the word negative suggest a counterproductive value while the perspective of the cynical attitude person can be valuable to a group.

Cynical people have the ability to wake up on payday, with perfect weather, the prospect of a great weekend and still find things to complain about. The cynical attitudes are sometimes more difficult to be around because they complain more, criticize more, gossip more, and whine more than any other group. However, cynical people are not bad people. They can be tempered and controlled to a certain extent to work adequately in groups.

It may be difficult for cynical people to find a high degree of contentment, and cynical people are usually less than pleasant to be around. Cynical people, however, can still be ethical people able to perform positive actions. Attitudes may influence, but actions are still the demonstration of character. Leaders who generally have a cynical of negative attitude, however, are rarely successful. Attitudes are reflective of leadership, and a person with a cynical disposition will not energize and influence people to their best work. Leaders need to understand the attitudes of their group, but they need to aspire to be optimistic in their demeanor.

The cynical attitude person can actually be valuable to a group, if the dynamic of attitude is understood. When leading or working with a group of positive, highly motivated people, the cynical attitude person can be a great help in providing a more complete point-of-view. They are realist and experts at telling why things cannot be done. This can add a degree of perspective to the group and help increase visioning skills. Cynical attitude people can act as a controlling force to the "can do" outlook of the optimistic attitudes. The optimists are likely to go over the cliff before they slow down to see they have fallen…the cynical attitude person will tell the group the cliff is there.

Destructive Attitude's Influence

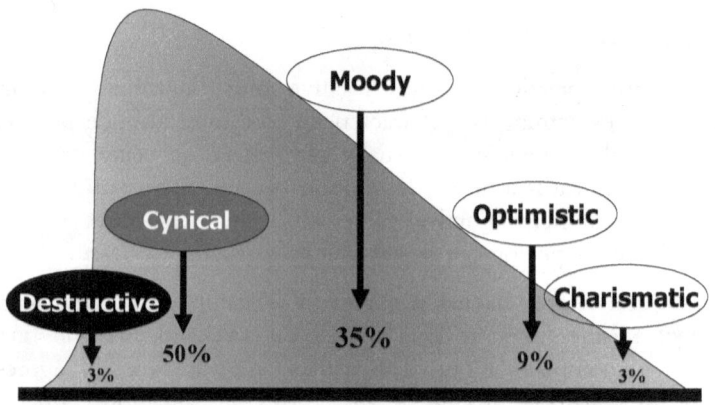

Characteristics of Destructive People

Moody, optimist, and cynical attitudes can have constructive and diverse roles in helping a team succeed. Moody attitudes are always changing dictated by external factors they perceive as beyond their control, the optimist is looking at the positive aspect of every situation, and the cynical is telling everyone why something cannot be done. Cynical attitudes, though often unpleasant to work with, do not generally hurt organizations but those creating negative attitudes in others do. Destructive attitude people have lower character elements of assurance, attitude, and actions and they affect groups in a disastrous way.

Destructive attitude people cripple a group's effectiveness by inhibiting communications, casting doubt, encouraging jealousy, and creating confrontations. Destructive people appear in all types of teams and seem to exist in almost every group. Destructive attitudes must be recognized, identified, and understood. Strategies must be developed to neutralize their affect for a group to have a chance to succeed.

Destructive attitude people are critical and suspicious of other people and their motives. Destructive attitude people are self-centered and often forfeit group goals to fulfill their personal agendas. People with destructive attitudes compete instead of learn. They mask any mistake by blaming others. They are not interested in improving their own performance but instead disrupt, destroy, or attempt to discredit the work of others. Worst of all, they influence the moody attitudes to a more cynical outlook, which hurts group morale.

These people are manipulative in their communication style and create much of their negative energy by distorting or misusing information. **(See Chapter 15, Dynamic of Communication)** Experience has taught them that being manipulative gets results they like. Destructive people rarely operate in the open but instead recruit and use operatives. Find the people in the organization who are orchestrating the misinformation and they are likely to be destructive attitude people. Open communication is the only way to force destructive attitudes to operate out of the shadows.

Unmasking the Wizard

Destructive people are often difficult to identify in organizations. They are like the wizard in the *Wizard of Oz* story. The wizard appeared to have a great deal of knowledge, power, and influence. He operated in a shroud of mystery; cloaked by a curtain and using a powerful voice while appearing to be the great wizard. He is not seen, but everyone is convinced the wizard is wise and all knowing. Dorothy, the Scarecrow, the Tin Man, and the Lion are convinced nothing can happen without the wizard. It is believed the fate of the group relies on this great wizard located in Oz.

The wizard sends characters on useless quests, which causes a great deal of fear, guilt, and stress hiding his inability to really help the situation. Later the wizard is uncloaked. The wizard is not great and powerful but is instead weak and incapable. He could do nothing for the characters they could not do for themselves. In the end, the wizard, who has manipulated Dorothy her whole stay in Oz, leaves her behind. She discovers her faith in him was unwarranted while she had the power all along to get back home.

Destructive people also have the ability to appear to have knowledge, power, and influence. They are experts at misusing information to appear this way. Like the wizard, they operate in a shroud of mystery. They like to be behind the scenes and invisible. Working out of sight helps them to maintain this illusion and

Destructive people are experts at misusing information.

keeps them from having to be accountable. Destructive people like to send people on "wild goose" chases. Creating fear, guilt, stress, and chaos makes them feel powerful and helps divert attention away from their disruption to the organization.

Like the wizard, destructive people are almost always found to be weak, ineffective, and pathetic when they are uncloaked and the illusion they have created of being indispensable is revealed. The fear and dread they have caused is found to not be reality. Many times the people they used have wasted a good deal of energy being manipulated. They send people off to fight "flying monkeys", causing fear, distress, and anxiety, when the people could have spent the same energy to accomplish something constructive. In the end, people discover destructive attitudes do not have any power over them...unless they let the destructive attitude influence them.

Identifying Destructive Attitudes

I once worked with a group that had been ravaged by destructive attitudes and had experienced a great deal of turmoil. By the time I started with them, the bedlam had pretty much ended, but I would often hear about "They" and "Them." "They" did this or that and what are we going to do about "them." One

Destructive attitude people only have power when others let them affect their attitude.

day, partly in jest, I asked one of the long-time employees who "they" were. The co-worker reacted with a little trepidation but also a little confusion and said, "We don't really know who 'they' are...but we fear 'them.'"

"They" exist in practically every organization and "they" have the same affect in all organizations. Improving the environment within an organization depends on finding out who "they" are and uncloaking the destructive attitude people effectively hiding out in organizations. People have the authority and responsibility to choose their attitudes. One strategy to improve group morale is to eliminate the words "they did" and "we can't." Destructive attitude people only have power when others let them affect their attitude.

Identifying destructive attitudes requires observation and analysis of not only what people are doing, but also why they are doing it. The first thing to observe is a person's self-image. **Destructive people have poor self-images.** They camouflage this lack of self-esteem by developing a synthetic or false self-image. Many times destructive people will appear to be arrogant and egotistical. Calling their actions into question results in a "how dare you question my motives" type of response. This synthetic self-image disguises their low opinion of themselves. Destructive people are also arrogant because they are extremely self-centered.

Destructive people gossip…it is their most effective tool. They are the people in the organization who know everything about everybody. Destructive people have an amazing amount of information about people in the organization because their energies are hardly ever focused on constructive activities. While others are concerned about work and outputs, the destructive attitude people are concerned about getting information they can use to stir the pot of controversy within the group. They are master manipulators.

They are the people who meet the new hires on the first day to "just fill them in about things." Watch any new person on their first day in an organization. Those who recruit people to be as negative as they are will be there. Destructive people rarely miss an opportunity to make a "new friend" and test to see how much influence they can have on that person. If you have people in your organization going out of their way to have a casual encounter with a new hire to tell them how things really work, you may have identified a potential destructive attitude person. This is not to say there are not good intentioned people wanting to make new people feel at home, but destructive people are interested in influencing and finding new people they can manipulate.

Destructive people are whiners and complainers. This might seem like an easy trait to identify but destructive people are experts at stealth. They are usually extremely cautious about who they whine to and are always looking for pawns to do the complaining for them.

The destructive attitude person's lack of self-assurance does not allow them to admit to mistakes. **Destructive people will never take responsibility** for their actions and are constantly looking for someone to blame. Casting blame and creating doubt are ways the destructive attitude person diverts attention from their shortcomings. **Destructive people cause chaos.** They usurp authority and fail to take responsibility **(See Chapter 11, Dynamic of Authority and Responsibility).** Often these people are purposely trying to undermine the people in the group that do have authority and responsibility for decisions.

Destructive people are defensive and suspicious. They have the ability to weave incredible conspiracy theories and they are convinced others are out to get them. A person constantly imagining intrigue and continually demonstrating an extreme paranoia about other people in the organization is probably working to get other people involved in their fantasy.

Destructive people doubt the motives of others, are dogmatic in their ideas, and are disinterested in seeing things from other people's perspective. More than anything else, **destructive people are critical.** They criticize co-workers, management, the organization, and practically everyone else. Destructive people usually have a "list" of people, groups, and things they do not like. That "list" will most likely include just about everyone but the person they are talking to at the time. Encountering someone who is chronically critical of others is probably the best indication they are destructive.

Remember, destructive people go well beyond whining, complaining, gossiping, and displaying other negative tendencies. They are influencing other people and using other people to affect the attitudes and dispositions of as many people in the organization as possible.

Dealing with Destructive Attitudes

After identifying destructive people, strategies to treat their effect on the organization must be developed. It is important to understand there are many more cynical people and moody people in an organization than destructive people. Many times the destructive attitudes are hidden while the cynical and moody people are used to cause disorder in the organization. Remember there is a constant contest for the attitude, outlook, and disposition of the moody attitude people.

Destructive people use manipulation, coercion, and misinformation. The "rumor mill" is one of their primary instruments in influencing the group's morale. Developing open communication **(See Chapter 15, Dynamic of Communication)** is essential in taking influence away from destructive attitude people. They are masters of using bits and pieces of information to motivate others. Destructive people can put two and two together to make five or any other answer that fits their motives. Developing a positive environment, which fosters open communication and exchange of information, can help neutralize the effects of the negative outlooks promoted by destructive people.

In the thirteenth chapter of Matthew in the Bible, Jesus uses a parable to describe a great strategy to effectively deal with destructive influences.

> *"The kingdom of heaven may be compared to a man who sowed good seed in his field: but while men were sleeping, his enemy came and sowed weed among the wheat, and went away. So when the plants came up and bore grain, then the weeds appeared also. And the servants of the householder came and said to him, 'Sir, did you not sow good seed in your field? How then has it weeds?' He said to them, 'an enemy has done this.' The servants said to him, 'Then do you want us to go and gather them?' But he said, 'No; lest in gathering the weeds you root up the wheat along with them. Let both grow together until the harvest; and at harvest time I will tell the reapers, gather the weeds first and bind them in bundles to be burned, but gather the wheat into my barn.'"*[14]

Like many teachings of Jesus, this parable has many diverse and deep meanings. The story, however, can be used as an example of dealing with destructive attitude people. In the story, the damage is done in secret "while men were sleeping." Destructive people

---

[14] Matthew Chapter 13 Verses 24-30, Revised Standard Version

often operate in secret and they are often hard to detect. After the spreading of unwanted seed, the householder shows wisdom and patience by not allowing the servants to gather up the weeds while the field was in production. Many times destructive people spark a witch-hunt, which damages the operation and functioning of the group. When this happens, people develop paranoia about the hidden actions occurring in the group. Soon more damage and disruptions are done. This search for the destructive people helps accomplish what they want...confusion, chaos, and anarchy.

The man in this parable demonstrated one crucial characteristic in dealing with destructive attitudes...patience. Many times leaders and other people in the organization must wait for the results of destructive behavior to be revealed and to let the group decide which attitude is best for the common good of the group. Effective leaders need to make people more accountable and responsible by documenting behaviors and performance.

Waiting for destructive attitude people to expose themselves can be a long and painful process. Destructive attitude people are like a cancer to the organization. They may require treatment or they may need to be removed. Dealing with destructive attitudes will require effort. Failing to recognize and treat the situation will prolong the pain in the organization.

After showing patience and letting the results become more apparent, the man in the story separated the weeds from the productive crop. Many times in dealing with the destructive attitude people, it is also necessary to separate them from the rest of the group. Sometimes this means taking influence away from the destructive people and sometimes it means terminating their association with the organization.

Dealing with and neutralizing the impact of destructive attitude people requires:

1. **Identifying them**
2. **Opening communication in the organization**
3. **Being patient in revealing their affects**
4. **Isolating or separating them from others in the group.**

One other effective strategy in improving attitudes and environment in an organization is to encourage and develop the most positive influence...the charismatic attitude, which creates positive outlooks and energy in other people.

Characteristics of Charismatic Attitude People

What organizations and groups of people need is the rarest of all the attitude archetypes, the **charismatic attitude**. Charismatic attitude people, by the definition used in this model, are not super-charged individuals who motivate and inspire the masses. Charismatic attitude people simply have the ability to create positive attitudes in other people…they are the encouragers. Charismatic attitude people have a strong self-image. They also have the ability to blend the idealism of the optimistic attitude with the realism of the cynical attitude.

Many times these people are quiet and unassuming. They are great listeners. Organizations wanting to improve need to identify and develop the charismatic attitudes. Charismatic attitude people help lift the outlook and attitudes of everyone, particularly that big group of moody attitude people embedded in every team.

Charismatic attitude people have the ultimate traits promoting success. They tend to be **self-assured** with a healthy self-image. Their confidence and assurance in themselves permit them to be **innovative**, **enthusiastic**, **caring about other people**, and **positive**. The charismatic person goes beyond having a positive attitude. They also inspire positive energy and emotions in others.

These people are fearless and draw strength by their own feelings of self-worth. Charismatic people tend to be visionary, goal oriented, and achieving. They frequently are humble because their high level of self-assurance allows them to be empathic to the needs of others and allows them to encourage other people. Charismatic people will attempt to make people better than themselves and in doing so prove that they are the best people to have around.

Becoming More Charismatic

Developing a charismatic attitude begins with high levels of self-assurance and self-actualization. Charismatic people focus on the "why and how" of situations. They are able to look beyond the obvious and think about the reasons and dynamics behind observations. They train themselves to not compete with others but to learn from others. They instead compete with their own best work. More than anything else, charismatic people are humble, meaning they put the needs of others before their own needs.

It may be impossible to have the perfect charismatic personality and attitude in all specific situations, but everyone should have the goal of becoming more encouraging and being a positive influence on the people with whom they come into contact. Being an optimist can be helpful to the functioning of a team, but creating positive attitudes in others is needed to really change the culture of a group and motivate individuals to high levels of accomplishment.

Charismatic people are choosy in their association with others, whether it is social or professional. They know the power of synergy, diversity, and encouragement. Charismatic attitudes will seek to find people on whom they can have a positive influence. They will also look for people who will have a positive influence on them. Charismatic attitude people will avoid situations where they will have little chance of positively influencing others or where others will have a negative influence on them. Charismatic attitude people look for opportunities to encourage and motivate others to do their best work.

Key Points

- Take authority and responsibility in choosing your attitude.
- Understand the differences in attitude types and how to use that diversity.
- Identify and deal with Destructive Attitude people in the group. Look for people who:
  - have poor self-images
  - gossip
  - interested in influencing and finding new people they can manipulate
  - are whiners and complainers
  - will not take responsibility
  - doubt the motives of others
  - are critical
  - are defensive and suspicious of others
  - cause chaos
- Become a more Charismatic attitude by building up others...be in the encouragement business to be a more effective leader.
- Count your blessings. Recognize the positives in your life, and realize any negative challenges are learning opportunities.

Chapter 15
Dynamic of Communication:
Developing Open Communication

"The purpose of communication is to inquire, inform, and persuade. If you spend more time inquiring and less time informing you can persuade more."

Effective communication is the best strategy to improve organizational performance, resolve conflicts, manage destructive attitudes, and deal with difficult people. Communication is how individuals and groups share ideas, influence, and learn. Developing a learning attitude as opposed to a competitive attitude is important to communicate at the highest level possible.

Poor communication is a common complaint in most organizations. Communication problems occur at all levels from upper management to front-line workers. Communication barriers are hard to identify and treat because people and personalities are involved. Separating the personalities from the dynamic often becomes the challenge.

INFORMATION FLOW

Flow of information presents a big communication challenge. Too little, or too much, information flowing through the group creates barriers in developing a positive work culture. It is impossible to have perfect communication. The limits of time restrict our ability to know every detail of information that we might get from another person. The goal is to get enough of the most pertinent information while filtering out the pieces of information that are not relevant to our decision making. These imbalances of too much or too little information need adjustment by understanding and utilizing the communication strategies used by individuals and groups.

The flow of information, which happens by communication, is the life-blood for an organization. The circulatory system of the human body has many similarities to the information flow in an organization. The heart, through a system of arteries, blood vessels, and capillaries, pumps blood through the body. Blood then travels back through the system to the heart again. Communication also flows through an organization. In the circulatory system, blood goes throughout the body then comes back. It is circular in nature, going out into the body and back to the heart again. Communication must also be circular in structure with information going out and feedback coming back. One-way communication, or a broadcast of information, is not effective in developing healthy, open communications.

Restricted Information Flow

If conditions in the body restrict blood flow or allow blood to flow outside of the system, it poses a serious health risk. Restricting the flow of blood deprives the body of oxygen and other nutrients needed for the normal functioning of the body. A restriction of information deprives the organization of the ideas and knowledge needed to operate at the most effective level.

One leadership challenge (although many leaders fail to see it) is a poor flow of information back to the decision-making level of the organization. Sometimes leaders surround themselves with "yes-men and yes-women" telling them what they want to hear. "Yes-people" are generally passive communicators but they can also be manipulative communicators withholding or misusing information for their own benefit.

At other times, leaders can be argumentative and confrontational. Insecure leaders may show little regard or enthusiasm for the ideas of others, especially when those ideas shatter their own illusions of the current reality. Messengers with bad news can become so intimidated by the reaction of the boss that information is simply not reported.

Organizations with a restricted flow of information struggle to keep up with market trends and have poor adaptive capability. They struggle to have a broad enough knowledge base to survive. Information tends to flow one-way in these organizations. Poor listening and little respect for other points-of-view characterize these organizations. A culture exists, which does not encourage open, direct, and honest exchange of ideas. Knowledge is power and those in charge tend to exert influence by hoarding information while disguising the real decision-making process.

Communication needs to be a two-way flow and the listener or receiver of information must also participate in establishing a culture for open communications. Every leader needs the courage and should take the opportunity to hear what people are really saying. Constructive, open communication can be an important tool in creating a vision for the current reality. **(See Chapter 2, Dynamic of Vision)** Leaders need to realize their position can be a barrier to open communications and they should seek ways to breach that barrier.

Hemorrhaging Information Flow

Another concern in the body's circulatory system is hemorrhaging, which means blood is outside the normal system. This loss of blood, if not contained, is fatal. In organizations, this hemorrhaging of information occurs when manipulative communicators misuse information by spreading half-truths, rumors, and innuendo to benefit their viewpoints.

Gossiping and the "rumor mill" cripple many groups and organizations. Solomon said, "For lack of wood the fire goes out: and where there is no whisperer, quarreling ceases. As charcoal to hot embers and wood to fire, so is a quarrelsome man for kindling strife."[15]

If the flow of information is not contained, it can do severe damage to the group, drain its energy, and create chaos. If the information system is hemorrhaging, the destructive attitude people and the manipulative communicators will be in power and control.

Organizations with a hemorrhaging information flow are often groups that are out of control. Chaos and confusion rule the information flow. These organizations are characterized by an overflow of information, usually unsubstantiated, confusing the direction of the group. The typical response by leadership to a group with a hemorrhaging information flow is to restrict the flow of information. This creates a vicious cycle of ineffective communication. When leaders try to restrict the flow of information, they ensure that information will flow outside of the traditional channels and when the information flow is out of control, a restrictive environment is likely to follow. When the flow is restrictive, it inevitably hemorrhages again.

---

[15] Proverbs Chapter 26 Verse 20, Revised Standard Version

Balancing the Flow of Information

Balancing and controlling the flow of information is vital in taking power and influence away from the destructive people in an organization. They depend on using and misusing information to create perceived influence. If the information flow in the organization is slow, it gives the destructive attitudes more opportunity to manipulate the bits and pieces of information they have.

People will get information. Using open communication and getting the information (good or bad) from the leadership to the whole organization is an effective way to reduce the effect of destructive attitude people. If the destructive attitudes are flooding the organization with false or misleading information, the group must have confidence in the reliability, accuracy, and value of information coming from leadership.

Balancing the flow of information is hard work requiring leaders to make continual adjustments. The goal of truly open communication is an ideal and no group of people will ever achieve a perfectly balanced open communication system. A commitment to improvement, understanding, and creating a clear vision of the current realities is the geniuses to balancing the information flow.

Learning versus Competing

Competition is common barrier to effective communication. Something about human beings causes competition, even over insignificant details. Our society trains and conditions us to compete with others. Competition is a powerful driving force, but competition becomes a barrier to effective communication.

Effective communicators, who are able to understand the dynamic of human behavior, learn how to change the programming in their minds. They train and condition themselves to have a **learning** mind-set instead of a **competing** mind-set. Competition is fine, and there is certainly a place for it when it comes to motivating, but a learning mind-set is essential in developing leadership potential and effectiveness. Learning means being self-assured enough to be wrong, to experiment, to enjoy life, and to view challenging situations as constructive instead of painful. Learning is about being open-minded, honest, and empathic. Developing this outlook, a mind-set of learning, helps a leader become an effective and influential communicator.

The purpose of communication is to inform, inquire, and persuade. Each person has a predominate communication style. One factor determining this style is a person's curiosity level or their learning attitude. People have a tendency to spend so much time trying to inform or persuade that they forget the most important part of communication: to inquire and learn. Moving from communication that defends a point-of-view to one that is seeking to understand is one way to improve organizational communication.

Dynamic of Learning in Communication

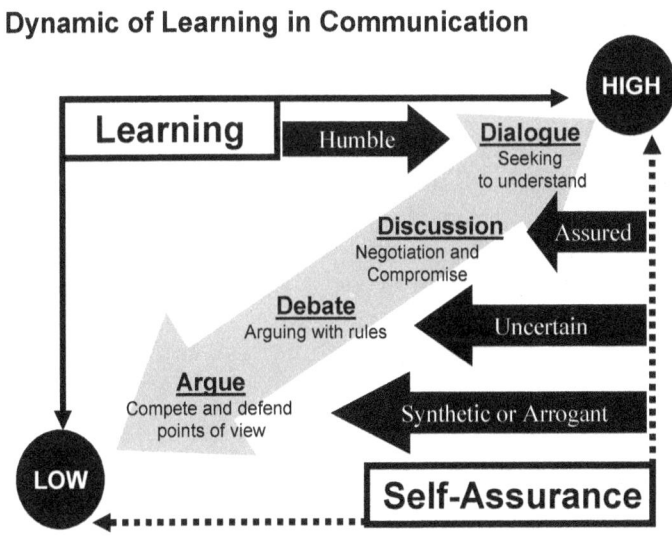

To **argue** is the least effective method of communicating when the objective is to learn and influence. The arguing style features low levels of self-assurance and curiosity. An argument usually occurs between two people or two groups of people, because arguments by their nature are a confrontation. Arguing is competing and defending a point-of-view. Understanding other perspectives or even discovering the truth is almost irrelevant in an argument. Arguments are about staking out turf and out maneuvering the opposition. Influencing the other party to change their way of thinking is just a delusion in an argument. The objective is to win and discredit the other point-of-view. Getting the other side to change their mind, agree, or compromise is not nearly as important as winning.

Sometimes arguments evolve, with rules and decorum, into a **debate**. In a debate, there is still a high level of competition and a low level of curiosity. Points-of-view are stated and defended. Respect for the other person and civility is greater, but winning the contest is still the prime objective. Political debates are a good example of how this process of communication works and what the purpose of this communication is to win and discredit. Imagine one of our modern political debates where one of the parties makes a point so simply, eloquently, and powerfully that the other side says "Great idea, we change our mind and we agree with you!" Generating ideas and constructive solutions is not the purpose of a debate…no one wins, they just defend and compete. Arguing and debating only serve to defend a viewpoint with little desire to see the other side.

Discussion is the most common type of communication and is more constructive than either arguing or debating. Discussion involves negotiation and compromise. The American system of government is designed on this principle of compromise. In a discussion, there may be many viewpoints represented. The sides still have their point-of-view they are trying to protect or promote, but in a discussion they are willing to "give and take" to accomplish goals.

Argument, debate, and discussion are all based on a competition mind-set and none of these styles are particularly concerned with learning, enlightenment, or truth.

The Greek philosopher Plato used and advocated a communication technique called dialectic, which can be defined as the art of investigating truth. In the dialectic, contradictory or apparently contradictory ideas are resolved by establishing truths on all sides rather than disproving one argument or the other. The dialectic thought requires open-mindedness, curiosity, and respect for other opinions. The modern word derived from the Greek ideas of Plato's day is **dialogue**. When using the dialogue style of communication, a person is not defending a pre-judged opinion. Communicating using dialogue is seeking to understand. When seeking to understand, we must suspend current beliefs and opinions in the search for truth. Seeking to understand means there is a possibility that our current ideas may be wrong.

Dialogue is the most open, constructive, effective, and difficult type of communication to use. A person must have an eagerness to understand a situation better; a willingness to explore their own and others' points-of-view; a desire to be curious beyond current knowledge; and seek to determine what is right and true. This outlook of learning instead of competing requires a high level of self-assurance and respect for the opinions of others.

Dialogue represents a genuine desire to understand a situation from another point-of-view. Communicating using dialogue calls for an appreciation for other peoples' experiences and knowledge. It leads to a greater perspective of the current reality by accepting the viewpoints of others. Communicating by dialogue, considers combined knowledge from many perspectives as necessary for a richer, fuller, and more complete understanding of the current reality. The goal of communicating through dialogue is to gain insight and usable knowledge.

Improving the ability to dialogue is a prerequisite to developing an open communication strategy in an organization. Again, the main ingredients of leadership are vision and influence. Learning to effectively dialogue will greatly aid a leader in getting all of the information and perspectives necessary to create a vision of the current reality.

Using dialogue or "active listening" can also help a leader be more influential. Active listeners do not tell other people what to do, give directives, or offer ultimatums. They ask questions and explore the attitudes, beliefs, and perspectives of other people. Active listeners know the value of information, but they also appreciate that people rarely argue with themselves. They have the patience to let others discover new ideas and willingly give up ownership of good ideas to others. Active listening and engaging in dialogue takes time and effort, but it is possibly the best single tool for a leader to use in influencing other people.

People who develop their ability to communicate at this level understand that each person, regardless of the person's background, has a unique point-of-view. This perspective is valuable in the pursuit of knowledge. Spoken words are only a partial representation of what a person thinks and believes. Words are only articulations of opinions, values, and beliefs. Words are adjectives for ideas. Dialogue demands exploring, questioning, and seeking in order to find truth, greater understanding, and wisdom. Using dialogue is the highest level of open communication and it reflects a person's self-assurance and respect for other people.

COMMUNICATION STRATEGIES

People, and groups of people, tend to adopt a communication style of **arguing**, **discussing**, or **dialoguing** depending on their **level of curiosity** and their **level of self-assurance**. Two other factors, the **level of influence** and **empathy** for others, also have an effect on the communication philosophy and communication strategies of people within a group. These four factors—influence, empathy, self-assurance and curiosity—determine a group's communication culture.

People in groups predominately use one of five communication strategies: **Argumentative, Passive, Negotiating, Manipulative**, or **Open**. Most people have learned to use a combination of these styles based on the situation. Effective communicators know how to identify and understand the communication style used by others and are able to influence the dynamic involved in communication in a constructive way to obtain positive results in an organization.

Argumentative

By nature, people compete. People are conditioned to think conflict equals a contest or confrontation. Not surprisingly, many people in our society use the argumentative or aggressive strategy today. By its confrontational nature, there is little hope of influencing anyone who takes an alternative viewpoint. Using an argumentative strategy consists of protecting points-of-view and contesting ideas opposed to those points-of-view. The argumentative strategy has little concern for other people, their ideas, opinions, or feelings.

> By nature, people compete. People are conditioned to think conflict equals a contest or confrontation.

Competition is the motivation driving this form of communication. The argumentative style is easy to implement because all a person needs to have is an opinion and a willingness to defend a point-of-view. Argumentative communicators are not interested in what's true, what's right, or what's better. They make up their minds then attack anyone who dares to disagree.

Dynamic of Communication Strategies

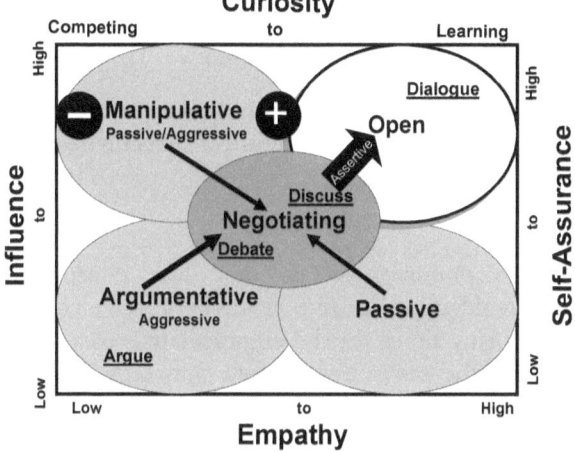

Cynical attitude people are often drawn to the argumentative strategy of communication. Winning, or perhaps more importantly seeing others lose, is an important element. Anger is a common component in the argumentative strategy. Many times, groups find themselves mired in argumentative communication situations even when there is no substantial disagreements.

Any little league sport is an interesting study in human behavior. It is an extremely difficult period when parents come face to face with the fact their children are just as average as they are. Competition is fierce. Not among the kids but with the parents on the sideline. Few Super Bowls, World Series, or Final Fours have as much riding on them as a little league game because the egos and the most primal urges of competition are at work. The super-charged emotions and the desire to see your kid do well restrict the ability to see things objectively for what they are.

Little league is also an excellent place to observe the argumentative style of communication. The purpose of the activity, to let kids play and have fun, becomes irrelevant to the competition. Many parents will say and do almost anything to defend the honor of their offspring. The pressure on the children to do well and justify the parent is sometimes overwhelming. Anger is a common sight at these events while objectivity and open-mindedness is not even attempted. Watching a little league event when your child is not involved is like being in a different dimension. The lack of objectivity and irrational views become comical. This competitive spirit blocking objectivity happens not only in little league, but also happens in all types of groups practicing argumentative communication.

Argumentative communication is a common experience and it is an easy style to participate in, but it is certainly not an effective communication strategy.

Passive

Passive communicators do not like confrontation and particularly avoid argumentative situations. Passive communicators compensate many times for the argumentative communicators by trying to keep the peace and smooth things over. They may be quiet and shy but many times passive communicators are outgoing and friendly. They may be talkative and seem to express themselves, but the main characteristic of passive communicators is that they keep things to themselves to avoid confrontation.

People who use passive communication strategies have a high empathy and concern for others. Often their concerns about what others might think of them makes them hesitant to share their thoughts, feelings, and perspectives. Unfortunately passive communicators (by their high concern for others and ability to listen) have constructive ideas, which rarely are shared with the group. Their ability to positively influence the group is thus restricted.

Passive communicators will usually just "take it" whether it is verbal abuse from co-workers, a lack of respect from superiors, or apathy from the organization about their views and outlooks. When confronted by a bully or argumentative communicator they will run away, ask for a transfer to another area, and avoid conflict at all cost. Unfortunately, passive communicators will find argumentative people in any group they join.

Several years ago, I was involved teaching a class using a management simulation. In this class, the participants were assigned an assembly process to work with and improve. There were several bottlenecks and problems designed into the simulation. The challenge for the participants was to find and solve these problems. People taking this class were typically professional people (managers and engineers) who had expert knowledge in their field.

During one of these classes, we had a person identify the problem and suggest a solution within the first hour of the eight-hour class. This person shared his opinion, which the group ignored. He then demonstrated passive communication characteristics. This person caused no problems, participated in all the activities, and seemed to enjoy the class. He had the answer needed by the group all day long and was unable or unwilling to express his ideas. Although he had high concern for the opinions and ideas of others, his inability to use communication as a vehicle to express ideas and persuade others, made him an ineffective in terms of communicating and sharing ideas.

Manipulative

The opposite of passive communication is the manipulative communication strategy. The passive strategy has high empathy for others and low influence. The manipulative strategy can have low empathy for others and a higher degree of influence. Influence, however, can be positive or negative. Manipulative communicators can also be positive or negative depending on their respect for the ideas and feelings of others.

Negative Manipulative Communicators

Destructive attitude people are masters of negative manipulative or passive-aggressive communication strategies. Their selfish outlook, their ability to create negative attitudes in others, and their desire to generate confusion, chaos, and diversions in the organization make the manipulative strategy a tool to mask their own shortcomings. Negative manipulative communication does more to harm the effectiveness, harmony, and morale of an organization than any other communication strategies.

Negative manipulative communicators, sometimes called passive-aggressive, have a wide variety of tactics in achieving their high level of influence. These communicators are experts at scheming and using other people to attain their objectives. Many times manipulative communicators are hard to identify because they like to work "behind the scenes" and in secret.

Using and misusing information is another tactic in negative manipulative communication. The truth, or its relevance to the good of the group, is not important to the negative manipulative communicator. This type of communicator is expert at putting bits and pieces of information together and weaving them into their own version of the truth to fit their purposes. Gossip and the rumor mill is their domain and many of their conversations will contain the phrases, "Did you know?" or "Have you heard?" Negative manipulative communicators are very calculating in dispersing information. They many times hold on to a damaging piece of information until it can best serve them.

Another characteristic of negative manipulative communicators is their ability to use or appear to use the other types of communication to accomplish their objectives. Negative manipulative communicators are expert arguers. Their purpose in arguing, however, is not to defend a point-of-view but to anger and incite emotions, usually against another person. They are also shrewd negotiators and since they only pretend to have a respect for the needs of others, they often come out better in the compromise. Negative manipulative communicators can also be passive, which means they will rarely share their real feeling, beliefs or attitudes. They will sometimes appear to be passive communicators but they are conniving and are usually plotting a strategy.

When a person in the group does something the negative manipulative communicator does not like, the manipulative person will not seek to understand the person's perspective. They will not directly confront or question the other person and many times the other person may even think they have a good working relationship.

> **Whining, complaining, and tattling are characteristic of negative manipulative communicators.**

Negative manipulative communicators rationalize their behavior by assuming other people interact at their selfish and scheming level. The negative manipulative communicator will often work behind the scenes and organize a "coup d'état" against the people they perceive as the enemy.

Whining, complaining, and tattling are all characteristic of negative manipulative communicators and phrases like, "It doesn't really bother me but..." and "I just thought you should know" are common. Negative manipulative communicators are dangerous to the performance, morale, and attitude of the group. The damage negative manipulative communicators have on the organization is in direct proportion to their low level of concern for other people.

Positive Manipulative Communication

Positive manipulation would seem to be paradox, but manipulative communicators can be constructive when they have a higher level of empathy and concern for others. It is often hard to distinguish between manipulation and effective management. Most good managers, have the ability to structure controlling forces and driving forces to manipulate individuals within a group to achieve group goals. Positive manipulative communicators come closer to the ideal of open communication style when they are less selfish, and have a higher interest in the welfare of others.

Once I worked for an organization, which had arranged to send me and another employee out of town for training. We had made plans, adjusted our schedules, and were looking forward to the trip. The day before our trip, an emergency happened at work and everyone had to cancel leave, as well as training, to help solve the problem.

The other person's boss informed him, in an authoritarian style, that the training was off and he "would not be going under any circumstances." The information was shared and the orders were given with little regard for the employee's thoughts or feelings. "You have to" is never a very powerful motivator unless you're looking for an argument. This supervisor kept the employee in town, but lost future influence as a result.

My supervisor used a different approach…a positive manipulative style of communication. He told me "Something has come up. I know you have been planning for a while to go to this training, but your one of my most positive and valuable people. You're innovative and have good ideas and if you can, I really need you here." What was I to do…I was obviously so valuable that I couldn't help but stay!

The reality is my friend was smarter and more valuable than I was to the organization. I'm sure I really didn't have a choice either. If I had refused to cancel my plans, I am convinced my supervisor would have reverted to the authority he had to make me stay. I know I was manipulated, but it sure felt good. My supervisor had high concern for the feelings of a new employee and took this negative opportunity to encourage me.

Leaders understanding the dynamic of driving force and controlling force can use this type of communication to structure and influence a group to constructive ends.

Negotiation

Using the negotiation or discussion style of communication incorporates more respect and consideration for other points-of-view. Moving a group to a negotiation strategy is the gateway to developing a more open and effective communication strategy. It is also much more effective at influencing others than an argumentative style, is better at bring out ideas than the passive strategy, and is much less destructive than the negative manipulative methods of communication used by destructive people. This type of communication allows parties to state their perspective then discuss what they like or do not like. Often this style involves trading off ideas and compromising.

Communicating by negotiation is like dealing with an economic system. There is opportunity cost, which means something of value is usually sacrificed in order to get a consideration for something else of value. There is also equilibrium because the sides are constantly adjusting their beliefs and the value they put on those beliefs as they come to agreement.

Negotiation incorporates listening to other ideas, but usually for the purpose of finding out what the other side has or wants. Strategies are then developed to get the most concessions from the other viewpoint. In this type of communication, the preconceived ideas are pretty well established. There is little effort to compromise beyond what is necessary. This form of communication often has many of the same competition characteristics of the argumentative style and sometimes reverts into the argumentative domain.

Parents who have experienced sibling rivalries have seen the negotiating style of communication up close. No matter how hard you try, nothing ever comes out exactly even. One child is constantly negotiating for more fairness…at least from their point-of-view. Parents find a great deal of "quality time" is spent refereeing these negotiations and trying to find a solution everyone can live with.

Nowhere is this role of mediator more apparent than when you take the family out for dinner. Mom wants to go somewhere quiet, where she can relax and enjoy a meal. The son wants hamburgers and the daughter; well, she wants the opposite of whatever little brother wants. The negotiation begins by listing all of the possibilities time and finances will allow. After a while, usually with some flirtations with arguing, the family choses a restaurant. Not everyone is completely happy, but everyone has had input and a decision is made.

Many managers take on the role of parent every day in the workplace. They are continually arbitrating disputes. They create suggestions and solutions for possible compromise. They think they have had a productive day if no one gets into an argument. The negotiation style of communication is generally more effective than argumentative, passive, or negative manipulative communication strategies, but it demands a lot of time from everyone, particularly managers and decision-makers. The constant demands of negotiation rob organizations of valuable time and energy, which could be used in dealing with new challenges and opportunities for the group. Effective leaders will strive to develop a more effective open communication strategy using assertiveness.

Open

Open communication strategies are the hardest to develop in an organization but they are also the most effective strategy for group and individual communication. Open communication involves using and developing the dialogue style of communication where an open and free exchange of ideas and opinions can occur. An open communication strategy and system is an organization's only real solution for destructive attitudes.

Developing open communication involves leadership and usually a change in the culture of a group. The group must encourage an outlook of exploring and respect for others. An environment must be nurtured promoting experimentation and innovative ideas while allowing for failure and mistakes. Open communication strategies are not concerned with knowledge of the past but with the challenges of the future.

The open communication style features the highest empathy for other people and has a high level of influence. This communication style demands individuals be self-assured and able to accept criticism. Open communication in an organization is characterized by direct and honest exchange of information as well as a willingness and aptitude by individuals to be assertive in sharing their ideas.

Most groups do not communicate openly. People have a tendency to let a wall develop between what they really think and what they are willing to share with others. People let fear (the fear others will not like them or their ideas) become a barrier. In most communication situations, two conversations are going on, the one in the mind and the other out of the mouth.

In the early 1980s, a T.V. show starring Tom Hanks and Peter Scolari call "Bosom Buddies" demonstrated this "dual dialogue" between what is thought and what is said. In this particular episode, the characters were at a restaurant on a double date with two distinct dialogues going on. First you heard what the characters were really thinking, which was stated by narration, and then you heard what they actually said. The differences between what was said and what was thought were hilarious. Many times the characters would say the exact opposite of what they were thinking. This episode captured in a comic sense what happens daily in real life. People do not say what they really think and feel.

This same "dual dialogue" happens routinely in business meetings. In almost any type of group meeting, there are two distinct conversations. One of these conversations happens in public in front of a group. Here people tend to communicate ideas, which are less than candid, open, and assertive. Things said will be structured for affect. Sometimes the comments will be argumentative, or passive depending on the group and the situation. Most certainly, the conversation will be affected by the size and make-up of the group. The next conversation happens right outside the door of the meeting when people talk one-on-one and face-to-face. These individual conversations will still not be completely open, but the barrier of having to please many different individuals is less.

A correlation exists between the size of a group and people's ability to freely share ideas.

A correlation exists between the size of a group and people's ability to freely share ideas. The most open and honest ideas happen inside our own brains. We should know what we really think. When we talk one-on-one to another person, it is often easy to say most of what we are thinking dependent on how we perceive the other person's point-of-view, how much we trust that person, or if we like or dislike them. As more people are added to the conversation, however, the openness and honesty gets diluted as we struggle to find that balance between speaking our mind and tactfulness.

When conducting strategic planning meetings, I have found these dual conversations often occur. While facilitating discussions to establish group values, core beliefs, and find common purpose, responses tend to be "sugar coated" and structured to comply with group norms. It is very rare to find a group, which is able to open up and share the real concerns, challenges, and barriers to the organization's success. It is usually much easier to get information about the real situation of a group by talking to people one-on-one. This phenomenon is one reason networking skills are so valuable to organizational development.

Leaders of groups should always be aware of the dual dialogue of group meetings. They should realize the conversation in the hall outside the meeting is creating a different perception of reality than was shared in the meeting in front of the boss. There is a tendency to advocate ideas. This is a valuable skill for a leader, since leadership depends on the ability to influence. However, strong advocacy can be a barrier to an open communication strategy and developing a clear vision of the current reality. Leaders who think dynamically depend on knowing the driving forces and controlling forces. An open communication strategy that involves inquiry, candid discussion of the truth, and a learning attitude can help capture the reality of the situation.

Developing an open communication philosophy is not easy. It requires courage and a great deal of self-assurance from individuals in the group. The organization must be diligent in supporting open communications. It must invest time to get the group to believe this will be the accepted method of sharing ideas. A culture for open communication must be nurtured.

Open communications must be direct, honest, and sincere. Open communicators must also reflect a high concern for others including tact and empathy. Open communicators believe the knowledge of the group is a greater value than the knowledge and intelligence of any one individual. They know shared perspectives, cumulative knowledge, a free flow of information, and innovative ideas lead to greater knowledge and understanding. Opposing ideas do not mean a contest or confrontation. A synthesis of information and a search for the truth is the prime motivator in the open communication strategy. **Learning is valued over competing.**

DEVELOPING AN OPEN COMMUNICATION SYSTEM

Developing an open communication culture requires three basic elements, which must be demonstrated, modeled, practiced, and reinforced by leadership:

1. A direct communication mindset, which involves listening and reflection
2. Organizational integrity for the information flow
3. Creating a learning attitude instead of competing attitude in the group.

Direct Communication

A direct communication mentality means saying what you think, but thinking about the good of others. Most people would find a person who really told them what they thought, annoying, irritating, and rude. Open communication requires directness with the highest concern for the feelings, ideas, and welfare of the other person. People should say what they are willing to share with everyone. Conversations about other people when those people are not around should ideally be the same as when those people are in the room. Talking behind people's back is in the domain of the manipulative communicator and this activity will quickly quench open communication.

Organizational Integrity

Organizational integrity for the information flow is essential in establishing a culture for open communication. When leaders allow individuals to circumvent the information flow, trust is lost. For example, an employee comes to a supervisor to complain about another employee. Assuming there is not a legal, ethical, or safety concern, but just a general dislike for the other person or how they do things, it would be healthy in developing open communications to get both employees involved in a dialogue.

When a leader lets an employee complain, make accusations, or defame the other person without having to communicate with that person, there is a break in organization integrity for the information flow. Not only has one employee been permitted to use a manipulative communication strategy but that employee on a subconscious level will also lose some trust in the organization for letting them do so. The employee will be less likely to expose himself or herself to criticism, knowing how easy it is to talk behind someone's back and manipulate the information flow.

I once worked with two people, who did not get along and were always communicating in a range of negative manipulative to argumentative styles. The problems would always start with an e-mail, (non-direct, non-face-to-face communication) then escalate to the point where one would be in my office, then the other. One of the technicians would even watch my office and make a point to come in immediately after the other to question what was said, defend his point-of-view, and then explain why the other was wrong.

For a while, I thought I was doing the job of management and leadership because I solved the problems for them by negotiating settlements. I would often go to one and explain they would need to compromise because the other had low self-esteem. The other person's low self-esteem made them difficult to deal with because they could not afford to be wrong. The technician I was talking to would always agree and determine he could be the better person.

I would then go and repeat almost the same self-assurance speech to the other employee and work out a compromise, which would last about two weeks. Finally, I realized I was being used and manipulated by both. (In addition, I was actually being manipulative myself.) They unintentionally learned that problems they created, I would solve. Like children, they quickly learned that causing disagreement and challenging one another got them attention and usually a favorable result based on my effort.

In the end, organizational integrity was re-established by refusing to meet with one without the other being present. They could no longer talk about each other in secret in my office. They learned organizational integrity by example. When they came to my office, the other person was immediately called and we had a discussion about the issues…face-to-face. They also learned I was not going to solve their problems for them anymore. Any compromises or problems they had with each other could only be solved by them opening up their channels of communication.

Learning Attitude

Attitude can manifest itself in a number of ways within a group. Morale in the group can be positive or negative, upbeat or pessimistic. The individuals in the group can be resentful or grateful. All of these feelings represent various attitudes, or views of truth, the group values. In developing an open communication philosophy in a group, the attitude of learning instead of competing must be created.

Learning, not competing is extraordinary.

People are competitive by nature. Anytime a group of people is involved, competition for a variety of scare resources will take place. People compete for attention, for influence, and for prestige. Individuals with low concern for others and poor self-assurance will often be more concerned with the failure of others, than they are with their own success and achievement. Effective leaders need to be able to place value on learning and improving instead of competing.

Creating a learning attitude in a group means giving people permission to fail, as long as they learn from the experience. A learning attitude involves seeking, inquiring, and respecting the viewpoint and ideas of others. Most importantly, the leader must be able to demonstrate a learning attitude. The leader must be able to develop the talents in the group to maximize success. Leaders cannot be threatened by the success and increasing influence of subordinate members of the group. Leaders must be able to share credit and even be willing to give away ideas to others.

Leadership can develop a more open communication philosophy within the group by being direct and straightforward in sharing information, maintaining the organizational integrity of the information flow, and by creating a learning attitude instead of a competing attitude in the group.

COMMUNICATION DYNAMIC IN ACTION

The dynamic of communication is complex and fluid. People and groups do not use one strategy exclusively but instead are constantly vacillating and moving between each of the strategies. Most people use the communication strategy that has worked for them in the past. Breaking old communication habits and moving to open communication strategy is challenging. It may not even be realistic to communicate using the open communication strategy all of the time. The open communication philosophy and the ability to dialogue, however, is the ideal for which groups should strive.

The most effective leaders will be able to use all of the communication domains depending on the situation and individuals involved. People use a variety of communication strategies and are shifting between these communication domains constantly. The strategy used at any given time depends on:

- **a person's natural communication style and tendency**
- **the situation**
- **the trust people have in the other party**
- **the importance people place on the information**
- **the communication strategy that is approved, adopted, and accepted by the group.**

Using open communication requires a person to be completely honest and truthful. There is a fear factor creating a barrier making it difficult for individuals and groups to move into truly open communication. People may only be able to function in the ideal of open communication for brief periods. To be an open communicator all of the time would be utopian but probably not practical.

Leadership depends on influence. Effective communication is the key factor in creating influence. Leaders need to understand the dynamic of communication but must also use the dynamic to guide, control, and influence the group. They need to identify the predominate communication style of the group and individuals in the group. Leaders need to shape the communication culture of the group toward an open communication philosophy. As a practical matter, the leader should always be trying to move argumentative, passive, and negative manipulative communicators to a negotiating style. Getting the group to the negotiating domain is the foundation for moving toward the ideal open communication philosophy.

Creating inertia and focus is a primary job of leadership in many aspects of organizational development. It is also an important function in creating a culture for open communication. A leader must be able to analyze where the group is at in the communication dynamic and where individuals are at in the communication strategy. The first step is to move people out of the least effective communications domains: **argumentative**, **passive**, and **manipulative**, and move them to the **negotiator** or **discussion** level of communication. When the group is at this level, the leader will need to look for ways to break the barrier of fear, which limits how much the group is able to engage in open communication.

Symptoms of *Non-Assertive* Communication

- You have trouble saying no, even when you really should
- You feel people take advantage of you or "walk all over you"
- You have trouble keeping your temper under control
- You find it easier to talk about someone than to someone

Steps to Becoming More *Assertive*

1. Express Empathy
   Say something that shows your understanding of the other point of view. This shows that you're not trying to pick a fight.
2. State the Problem
   Factually describe your difficulty or dissatisfaction. Tell the other party why you need something to change.
3. State what you want or need
   Make specific requests for the changes you expect in the other person's behavior.
4. Write down your feelings
   Try writing down your feelings and key points, before talking to the other party. Try to be non-emotional, objective, and factual.

Assertive Communication

Assertive communication techniques are how groups move from the negotiation strategy of communication to a more open communication. Assertiveness is not always appreciated as a communication technique because people confuse it with being aggressive, argumentative, or dogmatic. Many of us are taught that we should always try to get along with others. If someone says or does something that we do not like, we tend to become passive and try to stay away from that person in the future.

Assertiveness is stating honestly and directly what is wanted or expect from another person. It is dependent on strong self-assurance and a sense that you are in control of your destiny. People who have trouble saying no even when they think they should, people who feel others take advantage of them, people who have trouble keeping their emotions under control, and people who find it easier to talk about someone than to someone are non-assertive communicators.

To become a more assertive communicator, keep the focus on the problem or issue and not on accusing or blaming the other person. Express empathy for the other person's point-of-view but honestly state your viewpoint and what you think of the situation. Assertive communicators use facts and data, not judgments or opinions. To be more assertive, express ownership of your thoughts, perceptions, and opinions. Often it is a good idea to put in writing your feelings, facts, and beliefs before verbally sharing them with others. This helps an assertive communicator to be more objective and less emotional. The most effective communicators will be able to balance assertive communication with tactfulness.

Effective leaders establish a culture valuing the free flow of information and ideas for the benefit of the whole group. They value diversity and understand creating vision requires them to get the view from as many perspectives as possible.

Key Points

- The purpose of communication is to inform, inquire and persuade.
- Effective communication is the best strategy to use against destructive attitude people.
- Primary factors affecting the communication strategy include:
    - Empathy (From Selfish to Selfless)
    - Influence (From Apathy to Interest)
    - Curiosity (From Competing to Learning)
    - Assurance (From Synthetic to Humble)
- **Other factors affecting which communication style is used at any given moment include:**
    - A person's communication style and tendency,
    - The situation,
    - The trust people have in the other party,
    - The importance people place on the information and
    - The communication strategy approved, adopted, and accepted by the group.

Chapter 16
Using Dynamic Thinking:
Practical Suggestions to Maximize Your Leadership Potential

Leadership influences others toward a preferred future. A small business owner trying to grow his or her company for the future, an elected official representing a constituency, or a team leader trying to align the activities of their group with the overall strategy of the organization are all involved in the activity of leadership. A teacher in a classroom, a co-worker who says an encouraging word, and even a grandmother who takes her grandchild to Sunday school, are also practicing leadership.

Leaders have varying degrees of responsibility depending on their scope of authority. Leadership is required in a myriad of situations and performed at all levels in organizations. Leadership styles can differ greatly. Some leaders are quiet and unassuming, while others can be boisterous and flamboyant. Some leaders are participatory and democratic, while others are controlling and dictatorial. There are no perfect models or methods of leadership. Leadership styles are shaped by personality, situations, and the makeup of a group, but the activity of leadership is fundamentally the same: *to see the reality of the situation and influence events toward a preferable future for a group.*

THINGS TO DO

1. Believe in Yourself

Belief is a powerful force. It begins with possibilities, matures with purpose, is unleashed when it stirs passion, and is manifested in actions. Believing in yourself and in your own self-worth is the genesis of leadership ability. The self-assurance needed for the leadership attributes of innovation, empathy, positive attitude, and humility comes from a strong belief in your abilities and your purpose. Believe in yourself, because no one else can do it for you.

January 3, 2001, the University of Oklahoma football team won their 7th national championship at the Orange Bowl in Miami,

Florida against Florida State University. Oklahoma entered the game a 10-point underdog. During the previous five seasons, this team had a dismal record of 24 wins, 32 losses, and 1 tie.

Bob Stoops was hired in 1999 to turn the football program around. What his team was able to accomplish surprised many people in the football world. Matt Hayes from the Sporting News wrote,

> *Stoops has no ties to the tradition at Oklahoma, but he has an unmistakable crimson-and-cream aura. In just two years, Stoops has made* **believers** *of everyone associated with the program. Most important, he has his players* **believing** *they can accomplish anything.*
>
> *"He has them* **believing** *they can win," says Florida State coach Bobby Bowden. "That's where the battle is won."*
>
> *"The kids* **believed** *in the scheme because we had a guy who won a championship doing the same thing four years ago," says Brent Venables, Oklahoma's co-defensive coordinator. "They* **believed** *in us from day one, and that's a credit to Bob and what he has brought to this program."*[16]

Many factors go into winning and leadership; hard work, good luck, desire to win, and quality preparation. The power of belief resulting from self-assurance is a special attribute taking people to higher levels of achievement. Most experts before and after the Orange Bowl game felt Florida State had better players but the power of belief is a powerful force.

2. Be sure enough in yourself to be wrong…and be willing to change

Self-assurance gives a leader the ability to be wrong. Leaders are decision-makers. They are often required to make decisions based on partial or incomplete information. Sometimes a leader makes choices others will second-guess or criticize.

Other times, a leader will be forced to make decisions based on knowledge, which cannot be shared with other members of the group. For example, a manager might need to take disciplinary action against a popular employee involved in substance abuse. The details will need to be confidential for the good of all concerned.

---

[16] Hayes, Matt. "Sooner Rather Than Later." <u>The Sporting News</u> January 9, 2001

The employee is unlikely to give the real reasons for the manager's decision and is likely to even fabricate other reasons and excuses making his or her treatment seem unfair. This is often the price of leadership.

Sometimes leaders just make a bad choice and are wrong. Self-assured leaders develop an attitude of learning instead of an attitude of competition. One of the best teachers I ever knew was able to answer a question in class by saying, "I don't know, but we'll find out," while another less assured instructor would have tried to bluff his or her way through.

The great American inventor Thomas Edison allegedly said, "If I find 10,000 ways something won't work, I haven't failed. I am not discouraged, because every wrong attempt discarded is just one more step forward...." In George Bryan's *Edison the Man and His Work* Edison said, "The electric light has caused me the greatest amount of study, and has required the most elaborate experiments. Although I was never myself discouraged or hopeless of success, I cannot say the same for my associates."[17]

Being a leader takes courage; the state-of-mind enabling one to face fear with self-confidence and resolution. Being a leader requires responsibility. A leader must take responsibility for their actions but also for the performance, actions, and attitude of the group.

The ability of a leader to fail, to learn, and to improve comes from within—from the self-assurance a person develops over a lifetime. Failure is rarely permanent when a person has an attitude of learning and takes the opportunity to change and improve.

3. Think Positive

Attitude is a filter determining how a person feels about the things happening to and around them. It is a mental function affecting how people think and feel about various stimuli.

Attitude is an invisible quantity not always directly seen but demonstrated in actions. Attitude is like radio waves that are not seen, heard, or felt. Radio waves are not perceptible by any physical means without a radio receiver. With a receiver, the nature and

---

[17] Bryan, George S. *Edison, the Man and his Work.* New York: Garden City, 1926.

content of the radio waves are revealed. Attitudes are not perceptible except by the actions and demeanor of people.

People chose their attitude. They can be cynical or positive, learning or competing, resentful or grateful. People are affected by how they think. Thinking positively gives a person more hope, more energy, more enthusiasm, and a better outlook on life. A healthy attitude is dependent on how comfortable people are about themselves. Self-assurance helps build a positive attitude and a positive attitude will in turn build self-assurance.

We make choices, and our choices make us. Our lives, in a very real way, are a combination of all the choices we make throughout our existence. People have great freedom in making their choices, but that freedom comes with the responsibility we must take for our own actions. Beyond this responsibility, we have for the actions we take; we also have control over our attitudes. Successful people choose their own attitude and limit the effect outside influences have on their attitudes, actions, assurance, and success. Successful leaders do not fix the blame; they fix the problems by accepting responsibility for their decisions and maintaining a positive attitude.

4. Live for Today

If positive attitude builds up the self-assurance required for leadership, fear and worry are the great destroyers of self-assurance and self-confidence. People fear many things and for a variety of reasons. Fear is sometimes rational but often irrational. The ability to handle fear will build assurance and confidence. Fear can be caused by almost anything, but most fear and worry is futile.

People worry about things happening in the past, things they regret, and chances they wish they could have again. One characteristic of time is the past cannot be changed. We can learn from the past and use the experience to avoid future mistakes, but worrying about things in the past is pointless and damaging to self-assurance.

A great deal of time is spent worrying about the future. We can plan for the future, develop strategies to deal with future problems, and prepare to meet the challenges of the future but worrying about the future is wasted energy. Fears are magnified when they are worried about instead of acted upon.

Ulysses S. Grant, the great northern general of the American Civil War had been a complete failure at almost every enterprise he had tried before the war. His training as a military officer at West Point, however, made him a valuable commodity at the beginning of the war. Grant was viewed as an average officer at the beginning of the Civil War but his ability to fight and overcome fear made him one of the real heroes of the war.

Grant related an experience he had in dealing with fear early in the western campaign.

> *"As we approached the brow of the hill my heart kept getting higher and higher until it felt to me like it was in my throat. I would have given anything then to be back in Illinois but I kept right on. When the valley below was in full view I halted…the enemy's troops were gone. My heart resumed its place and it occurred to me at once that he had been as much afraid of me as I of him. This was a view of the question I had never taken before but it was one I never forgot afterward. The lesson was valuable."*
>
> General U. S. Grant[18]

Later, in the battle of the Wilderness, Grant was responsible for the entire Union war strategy. Like other Union generals, his first encounter with Robert E. Lee was a near disaster. Lee had rattled the army of the north and nearly cut Grant's supply lines. While most of the officers were shaken and talking about what Lee might do to them next, Grant was calm and told his staff to stop worrying about what Lee was going to do to them and think about what they were going to do to the enemy. This was a new attitude for the Union army and one that brought them victory. Grant's ability to overcome fear and be confident in the face of fear is a powerful lesson about the power of assurance.

While attending a conference in Baltimore, Maryland, I was able to spend an afternoon visiting a traveling exhibit of artifacts from the Titanic. The famous ship sank on April 15, 1912, in one of the greatest sea disasters with a loss of about 1,500 lives.

The great ship, at that time the largest and most luxurious afloat, was designed with a double-bottomed hull, divided into 16 compartments, with watertight bulkheads. Unfortunately, the

---

[18] Grant, Ulysses S., *Personal Memoirs of U. S. Grant*, Charles L. Webster & Company, New York, 1885

watertight bulkheads only extended 10 feet above the waterline, and could not seal the ship into completely separate watertight compartments. One of Titanic's architects estimated the damage amounted to only 12 square feet! The worst single puncture was probably a 3 to 4 foot hole with the majority of the damage in the form of a 3/4-inch gash. The water simply filled up one compartment, spilled over the containing wall and flooded another compartment.

Any four of these compartments could have been flooded without endangering the ship's buoyancy. Had the ship been built with true watertight compartments, it might have been as unsinkable as many thought it was on that night. The small amount of damage, spread over too many compartments resulted in disaster. People do the same thing with worry. Most people are usually not crushed by one catastrophic event. They let all those little holes linger and flood the many compartments of their life. Leaders need to control the damaging effects of fear and worry by living for today.

Jesus Christ spoke about the damaging effects of fear and worry when he said, *"Do not be anxious about tomorrow, for tomorrow will be anxious for itself. Let the day's own trouble be sufficient for the day."*[19] Learning to deal with the problems of today, without letting the worry they create spread into weeks, months, and years is one effective way leaders can deal with the negative consequences of worry...to live in airtight compartments.

Today is what leaders can impact the most. Yesterday's decisions are today's results, but tomorrow will be the results of the decisions and actions leaders take today. Leaders need to be able to learn from the past, plan for the future, but live for today.

5. Create Vision

Developing the ability to see things the way they really are, instead of how we think they are or how we wish they would be, is a good foundation to wise decision-making, effective planning, and leadership.

One of the basic premises for thinking dynamically is developing the ability to use inductive reasoning and gaining

---

[19] Matthew Chapter 6 Verse 34, Revised Standard Version

perspective on situations to provide a vision of the current reality. Developing a systematic approach to interpret information is one method to create a clear vision of the present.

Emotion, preconceived ideas, personality differences, lack of objectivity, time, and limited perspective are all barriers to seeing the current reality. Leaders are decision-makers and good decision-making is based on objective information. Often the value of a leader to a group depends on his or her ability to make good decisions. Emotions are a poor basis for making a decision.

Being a business owner is a challenging job and a big responsibility. Owners make decisions affecting their profitability and survivability, but these decisions also concern employees, business partners, vendors, lenders, and a score of other stakeholders that may be reliant on the performance of a business. Business owners and entrepreneurs put so much of themselves into their businesses; they often become emotionally attached to their business enterprise. This emotional attachment can make it difficult to see what the realities of the current situation are and make effective decisions for the future.

One thing most successful small business owners will do is to use the accounting tools like the Income Statement and the Balance Sheet to provide an objective view about the performance of the business. The Income Statement tells the business owner how much money the business is making or losing based on factual data produced by business transactions. The Balance Sheet is also an effective tool at summarizing the financial position of a company (comparing what the company owns compared to what it owes). These financial tools help a business owner make decisions based on more factual and objective information than opinions or feelings.

Leaders of all types of groups should be looking at tools to objectively measure the current situation. Learning to use the models in this book, collecting data, analyzing information, and developing other tools to get objective information are some methods leaders can use to create vision for the current reality to help make better decisions for a preferable future.

6. Be more self-less and less selfish

Selfishness is the root cause of conflict, jealousy, fighting, stealing, lying, and a host of other human shortcomings. Selfishness is the natural physical response for people. Maslow's hierarchy of needs showed that people are first motivated by survival, security, and safety. People compete for survival, but as we mature and develop as human beings we must evolve to higher order motivations; learning, higher concern for others, and selflessness.

Being selfless requires extraordinary levels of self-assurance. Humility (putting the social, physiological, and emotional needs of others first) is the highest level of self-assurance a person can possess. Being selfless is a challenging goal, but leaders must develop a high concern for others in the group. To build influence leaders need to share credit for accomplishments, protect inexperienced and developing members of the group, and demonstrate that the needs of the group outweigh the personal desires of the leader.

Selfish leaders may be able to have the position of leadership, but the more selfless leader will develop long-term influence for more powerful leadership.

7. Plan for Success

The purpose of planning is to begin with abstract ideals, desires, values, and dreams then transform them into concrete actions and accomplishments. Group planning needs leaders who can take the ideas generated by individuals in a group, and focus the energy of diverse personalities toward goals and objectives.

Leaders continuously guide people through the process of planning. Leaders are accurately establishing the current realities and available resources as well as investigating the changing needs of the people in the group. Realistic yet challenging goals keep a group's energies and efforts moving in a mutual direction toward aligned actions. Leaders may be involved in allocating resources of the group to help obtain established goals and they should be involved in delegating specific actions required to achieve progress for the group.

The dynamic of planning is constantly changing due to internal dynamics in the group and outside influences that are sometimes uncontrollable. Leaders are constantly adjusting the attitudes and efforts of the group to meet these evolving circumstances.

Apollo 13, with astronauts James Lovell, Jack Swigert, and Fred Haise, launched into space and toward a landing on the moon in April of 1970. Every detail of the mission had been carefully planned with a contingency for almost every conceivable problem. The inconceivable struck when an explosion in outer space damaged nearly all essential systems. The astronauts were more than 200,000 nautical miles out in space with a dead spaceship, including its main propulsion engine. The explosion had wiped out the main supply of life-sustaining oxygen and power.

The serious nature of the emergency was immediately evident to the crew and Mission Control. The carefully detailed planning of the past few months was useless, but new planning was evolving to meet the new realities.

The goals of this mission quickly changed from landing on the moon to one of survival. New solutions had to be discovered to meet these new challenges. Innovative ideas and untried solutions were necessary to meet the new current situation and the resources available due to the disaster. The ability of the entire mission team to adapt and adjust the planning process played a major role in the successful completion of one of the biggest possible failures in exploration history.

Leaders need to be able to use their skill in planning to prepare for the worst-case scenario. If a group can survive the worst, they can thrive through the best.

8. Demonstrate the Important

Most plans do not fail because there is a lack of imagination or ability to set goals. Plans fail when actions are not done to accomplish goals. In working with companies doing strategic planning, we will typically do some kind of activity trying to establish the core values and fundamental beliefs of the group. Invariably the group will say, "Quality customer service," is something we highly value for our organization. When the follow-up question asks them to list ways they demonstrate how they value quality customer service, groups often fall silent.

Beyond helping the group establish their purpose and their values, a leader must demonstrate those values and ideals. If a leader values open communication, they must demonstrate that openness is important by being honest and direct in their communication and not participating in gossip. If a leader says authority and responsibility must be in balance, they will need to demonstrate they are being responsible for the authority they have been given. Followers will not always listen to what a leader says, but followers will certainly watch what leaders do.

Leaders must demonstrate in actions, what is really important. To successfully complete the planning process, leaders will do the little things to accomplish the big things.

9. Do the Right Things, not the Easy

Doing the right thing is not always easy, but it is always the right thing to do. Personal integrity builds trust with a group while increasing influence, but it is also one of the most challenging things to do.

A recently hired school superintendent worked with a board of education. After a few weeks, some of the board members called the superintendent daily making suggestions about the operation of the school. Legally, a board only had decision-making authority when a quorum was present and the board was meeting in public session. These suggestions and ideas seemed harmless enough at first, but before long these few board members asked for certain personnel to be dismissed and preferential treatment given to some vendors.

The easy thing for the superintendent seemed to appease the board members; after all, they were likely to leave service in a few years anyway. In the short-term appeasement seemed easier. These new requests, however, violated the superintendent's sense of ethics and possibly violated the intent of the law. The superintendent refused to conduct business outside of the board meeting, despite threats and pressure from the board members. The situation became contentious and difficult.

In the long-term, the composition of the board changed. The school survived several exhaustive audits, proving the superintendent's fiscal responsibility. The short-term ordeal of standing up to board members not only earned this leader respect with the board, but also with colleagues and subordinates.

10. Don't worry about problems, solve them

Good problem solvers are analytical, logical, and objective. They do not let biases and prejudices keep them from seeing all possibilities. Problems are opportunities for leaders to build influence, because solving problems demonstrate competence for the leader while providing safety and security for the group.

Problems are also possibilities for innovations and improvement. Often a problem is a symptom signaling a need for future change. Sometimes the best solution to a problem is the most obvious. Problem solvers should be open-minded to all possibilities.

11. To get ideas implemented, give them away

The hoarding of ideas keeps most ideas from happening. The competitive nature of people often causes them to be protective and possessive of things, people, and especially ideas. Eric Hoffer was an American social philosopher. His work was original and completely out of step with dominant academic trends of the time. Hoffer was self-educated and avoided the academic mainstream and the straightjacket of established thought.[20] Hoffer said, "Our originality shows itself most strikingly not in what we wholly originate but in what we do with that which we borrow from others."

Ideas are like roses, they only work well when given away. Leaders are responsible for focusing the group's efforts in a collective direction and implementing new ideas is often something a leader must do. If a leader really wants to get an idea implemented, they will give it to someone else in a group.

Even argumentative people rarely disagree with themselves. People like to be involved and they like to feel important. Effective leaders know that it is always better to give people choices instead of directives.

I once observed a supervisor practicing the art of giving an idea away so expertly that the lesson always stuck with me. The supervisor had been given a direct order to implement a production change that was going to be unpopular with the group. Instead of going into the meeting and giving directives, which would have resulted in arguments and defending a point-of-view, he presented the problem and asked the group for solutions. After carefully monitoring the discussion, keeping the group on track, and brief brainstorming solutions began to be generated. Sure enough, one of the group members offered almost the same idea that had been directed by the corporate office.

The supervisor continued to develop the discussion and fostered ownership for the idea with the group. He finally concluded by saying, "That's a great idea, I think we'll go with it." At the end of the meeting, the group left with a positive feeling and

---

[20] http://www.freedomsnest.com/hoffer.html

some genuine excitement about the new procedure. I am confident when push came to shove the supervisor would have ordered the new procedure to be implemented, but by giving the idea away, he made his job easier and the group more productive.

12. Build the people around you

Old, but good advice, "Treat other people, the way you want to be treated." Perfectly followed, this golden rule would resolve most personal, professional, national, and international conflicts and disputes. Having the high degree of self-assurance to become more selfless and less selfish is central to ethical leadership.

Replicating talent is how leaders multiply effectiveness. Leaders should empower people to do their best work by properly preparing them to take high levels of personal responsibility. Transforming an immature group (one that depends on the leader to make all-important decisions, mediate conflicts, and direct activities in detail) into a mature group (able to function at high levels of authority and responsibility) requires developing personal responsibility. Leaders do this by understanding the driving or motivating forces and establishing the appropriate controlling forces. Leaders must motivate while setting the parameters of behavior to focus the energy of the group on positive goals.

Parenting is one of the purest forms of leadership. It fulfills the basic definition by providing influence toward a positive future and vision of the current reality coming from years of experience. Newborn babies come into the world helpless and totally dependent on the parent. As children grow, they become more self-reliant and assume more responsibilities. The parent will expect children to dress themselves, take responsibility for bedtime, and perhaps do simple chores.

As children become adolescents, they become physically more mature, but still need strong guidance from parents. Adolescents should be learning more and more responsibility, but parents by virtue of experience have a better vision of the challenges and opportunities of young adulthood. This training process for the parent can be quite demanding. Giving adolescent children responsibility can be painful. Although it might be easier in the short run for parents to clean the child's room, make all of the decisions, and fix all of their mistakes, responsible parents know that in the end children need to be prepared to provide for themselves.

By the time children mature to adulthood, parents who have properly trained and developed the child expect the child to be completely self-reliant. The job of leadership for the parent, however, is not over. Mature children may come to the parent for advice and wisdom, but the role for the parent is now one of advisor, counselor, and confidant instead of caretaker.

This idealistic model of the parent-child relationship demonstrates how people are trained, developed, and prepared. When parents do not provide this type of leadership, their neglected children are ill prepared to take responsibility and cope with the challenges of life result.

For the leader of any group, the process of development is similar. The leader will need to determine the maturity level of the group before deciding how much hands-on direction will be needed. The maturity of the group does not depend on the age of the people in the group, but on their ability to take responsibility.

Like parents, a leader will need to teach and develop people. They will need to delegate and give group members learning experiences. Leaders manage the learning process for personal responsibility by setting the tolerance for failure.

Like an adolescent child, this may be a painful process. Learning often involves mistakes and failure. Eliminating mistakes and reducing the stress and chaos of learning seems attractive in the short-term. However, failing to develop and empower people to take higher levels of authority and responsibility rob a group of future performance capacity. It is easy to fall short at this important developmental stage. Many leaders find it easier to be the problem solver and decision maker than the teacher and developer of personal responsibility. Leaders feel they cannot afford the time to let others learn. In the short run, this may seem productive, but the long-term perspective may result in a group unable to meet future challenges. Like adolescents, the group will likely not take responsibility unless they have been prepared for it.

Finally, a leader hopes to have a mature, self-reliant group. He or she will want the group to be able to overcome challenges and adapt to future changes. Leadership strives to develop individuals able to move beyond the basic need for survival, success, and security, and become a group doing significant activities. As the group reaches full maturity, the leader's role may change, like the parent of a successful, self-actualized adult child. The best leaders are looking to make other people better.

Leaders are in the people development business. Encourage, challenge, and prepare people and they can accomplish great things. People make up groups and organizations. The quality of the individuals in the group defines the quality of the group. The most effective leaders develop people by managing the learning process to teach personal responsibility.

FINAL REFLECTIONS

Change is inevitable and leaders should always prepare people for the challenges of tomorrow. People excelling at the art of leadership have an aptitude of seeing reality. They are able to create a vision of the future by understanding the current realities of the present. Visionary leaders value perspective and are skilled at examining **what is happening now** and determining **why it is happening**.

The ability to transform a clear vision of the current realities into action for the future through planning is another characteristic of effective leaders. The ability to take the abstract, individual opinions of the group and transform them in to aligned action only happens when leaders are able to focus attention on common goals and objectives…the purpose for the group.

Life is about making choices, about consequences and rewards. Many choices will require an ethical decision in leadership. Making the right decision is not always easy or expedient but doing and choosing the right thing is always the right thing to do. Integrity is rooted in a leader's elements of character: **assurance** in self, **attitude** toward others, and **actions** demonstrating values. Effective leaders succeed by understanding the **power of belief**, the **responsibility to choose**, and the **opportunity to change**.

LOOK FOR THESE OTHER BOB PERRY BOOKS:

The Broken Statue
Mimosa Lane
Brothers of the Cross Timber
Guilt's Echo
Lydie's Ghost
The Nephilim Code
Return from Wrath
WOBS: The Wisdom Of Bob
For the Greater Good
For the Greater Good: Abigail's Story
For the Greater Good: Redemption
Spiritual Renewal: Transforming the Mind

www.bobp.biz

www.ingramcontent.com/pod-product-compliance
Lightning Source LLC
Chambersburg PA
CBHW021423170526
45164CB00001B/73